Christian Prayer for Today

Christian Prayer for Today

FRANK WHALING

SAINT ANDREW PRESS
Edinburgh

To my family and Brian Hardy

First published in 2002 by
SAINT ANDREW PRESS
121 George Street
Edinburgh
EH2 4YN

Copyright © Frank Whaling, 2002

ISBN 0 7152 0765 2

British Library Cataloguing in Publication Data
A catalogue record for this book is available from the British Library.

While every effort has been made to verify the accuracy of previously published quotations and to obtain permissions where appropriate, the author will be pleased to rectify any omissions for future editions of this book.

Typeset in Caslon
Printed in Great Britain by Creative Print & Design, Wales

Contents

Preface

This is a book of daily prayers, covering a month, for Christians of all persuasions. Each day is divided into eight sections. An introductory sentence, setting the tone of the day's prayers, can be revisited throughout the day. The second section praises God, and the third section thanks God for all the facets of our lives. The fourth section focuses upon self-examination and forgiveness, and the fifth section opens up a theme for meditation and reflection. Prayer for oneself takes up the sixth section, and Prayer for Action in the seventh section combines praying for others and commitment to action on behalf of others. The eighth section is a sentence for contemplation at the close of the prayers that can be applied to daily life.

This eightfold division provides a kind of liturgy for proceeding through the main elements of personal prayer. As the Introduction suggests, each day's prayers can be read through briefly, or read through slowly, or worked through very slowly. More benefit is gained by spending more time. A set time and place each day is probably the ideal way of gaining most help and insight from the prayers; but the best way is what suits the individual. These prayers are a means to an end rather than an end in themselves. They are intended to encourage readers to set up a pattern of prayer for themselves. They are offered in the conviction that personal prayer is very significant.

It is understood that personal prayer is to be seen implicitly as part of a wider circle of spirituality. The communal prayers of the wider Christian tradition, prayer in smaller fellowship groups, family prayer, extempore prayer and liturgical prayer can all be part of the wider whole of the spiritual life. Moreover, prayer in its wider form encompasses the whole of life. It works itself out in social involvement, in work, home and leisure situations; it has to do with the kitchen and the bedroom. And yet personal prayer is usually the powerhouse behind other kinds of praying, and behind the whole of living. Prayer is an integral matter that is far wider in scope than private prayer; and yet personal prayer may well be for many people the effective trigger to vibrant Christian living and the lack of it a brake upon Christian effectiveness.

Nowadays, two themes tend to dominate the popular conception of religion. One is the importance of spirituality. A trip into any good bookshop will often reveal a whole area devoted to spirituality, including books on meditation, personal inward development, spiritual growth and so on. Many young people meditate outside the sphere of organised religion as part of their lifestyle and world-view. The Christian tradition (as with the major religions generally) is no longer necessarily seen as a vehicle of prayer and meditation, especially among the younger generation. The second, related, theme is the assumption that the Christian community, and indeed the other established religious communities, are somehow lacking in spirituality. The opinion is commonly offered that if it is spirituality you are searching for, the Christian tradition is not the place to start. In the popular imagination, this supposed lack of spirituality is a significant reason for the perceived decline of the church.

Clearly, questions can be asked about these popular presuppositions. The church may be declining in parts of Europe, but it is growing rapidly in southern Africa, Latin America, Oceania and parts of Asia. There is more spirituality in the church, and in the other major religions, than the world is willing to credit. Media hype, and the coyness of especially Protestant Christians about their own spiritual lives, feeds into this popular sense of spirituality being mainly outside the established religions. And yet this very perception, even if exaggerated, is surely a serious matter containing an element of truth.

In short, the renewal and revival of personal private prayer is not just a matter for individuals such as you and me, relevant and crucial though this may be; it is a significant element in the potential renewal of the Christian community in Europe.

I have been struck by the importance which the New Testament writers give to Jesus as a man of prayer. He is portrayed in many other ways too: as prophet, priest, king, healer, miracle-worker, Lord, Messiah, teacher and so on. But even a cursory reading of the Gospel of Luke makes clear the significance of prayer in and for the life of Jesus. His birth is anticipated by prayer through the insights of Mary, Zechariah and Elizabeth; his birth is steeped in prayer and recognised in prayer by Simeon, Anna and Mary. As a boy of twelve, he tells his anxious parents that they should have known he was all right, for he was in his Father's house; he was later to rebuke the money-changers for making his Father's house of prayer into a den of thieves.

Prayer features prominently in the story of his baptism and even more strongly in his temptations in the wilderness. Throughout his ministry, he withdrew to lonely places in order to pray. Before calling the disciples, he spent the night in prayer; in the garden of Gethsemane, he later did the same. Peter's statement about his Messiahship and the Transfiguration experience arose out of situations of prayer. The Lord's Prayer and some of the parables addressed the questions of how and why to pray. Jesus's final words on the cross included prayers. Luke's Gospel ends with Jesus leading the disciples out to Bethany and blessing them with uplifted hands, and it was in the act of blessing that he departed from them. Thus prayer was important for Jesus – and, in engaging in a life of prayer, we are following Jesus himself. Many of the prayers in this book are my own. I have also borrowed ecumenically from the whole history and the whole diversity of the Christian tradition. Most ages of the church and most traditions within the Christian community are represented, including contemporary non-western Christianity. Wider literature is present, including Shakespeare, Wordsworth and occasional passages from other religious traditions with relevance to Christian prayer. Passages are also included on subjects such as ecology, justice and freedom, global issues and so on.

Different modes of prayer are present, which becomes apparent in reviewing the whole work. This book is in various ways traditional, liberal and radical; it contains the evangelical, the mystical and the pragmatic. It crosses over boundaries that are sometimes kept separate. It accepts the reality of God, albeit on the basis that we can only know God inasmuch as we know ourselves. It accepts the complexity of human nature. It recognises the spiritual significance of the world of nature and the present ecological crisis. It admits a certain ineffability within the Godhead, within humankind and within the natural realm under God.

Eight modes of spirituality are present in this work. The first, relating to nature, we have mentioned already. This strand, although hinted at in the Psalms, the New Testament and St Francis of Assisi, is basically new in that it rejoices in nature as God's creation but also recognises the seriousness of the ecological dilemma that faces the world. Thus prayer has to do with nature as well as with human beings and the divine.

A second mode, often associated with the Quakers, relates to a spirituality of silence. Silence is assumed and provided for within the daily prayers. Silence punctuates the intervals between the different sections of prayer. Silence at the beginning centred upon the opening sentence is an important part of the whole process of prayer. It is not an absence of noise; it is a creative presence.

A third mode, taken partly from the Orthodox tradition, relates to the creative repetition of phrases. This applies especially to the opening approach prayer and the closing prayer of contemplation. The repetition of the Jesus Prayer is well known in the Orthodox community, in its various forms, for example 'Lord Jesus Christ, Son of God, have mercy upon me', and it is taken to be the case that this process can build up within the person of prayer the reality of what the words are saying. We may note in passing that creative repetition and silence can either alternate or be joined together.

A fourth mode is what we would now call a charismatic spirituality. Some of the hymns and pieces within the book are essentially outbursts of joy of devotional splendour. They are to be welcomed and used as such. They suggest a spirituality of ecstasy.

A fifth mode, associated at times with the Social Gospel, seeks to engage in active social involvement in the world. Prison reform, alleviation of poverty, help to refugees, succour to AIDS sufferers, social reform in general, better health and education, more fairness – those are its touchstones. This mode centres upon prayer for those in need, and the intention is to make social involvement part of active spirituality.

A sixth mode, which seeks to go beyond social involvement, may be seen as liberation spirituality. It has a deeper intensity. It cries out inwardly at the injustices of the world. It raises questions about basic matters such as the role of global capitalism in world poverty and ecological decay. This mode is used occasionally in the daily prayers, although it is usually related to one's own inward spirituality as well as to outward 'rage' at injustice.

Following on from this, a seventh mode relates to the spiritual world within and a spirituality of inwardness. This is common in various traditions although perhaps more obvious in Roman Catholic figures such as Julian of Norwich, John of the Cross and Ignatius Loyola. Some of the meditations in the book use an inward creative imagination to go back to be with Jesus in parts of his life and to open up a spiritual world within: to be there at the Pool of Siloam, at the healing of a leper, on the road to Jericho with the Good Samaritan and so on.

Finally, there is present in the prayers what, for want of a better term, may perhaps be called the global spirituality mode – although it seems to me that it is equally a radical Christian mode. This takes seriously the psychology of C. J. Jung, the work of Teilhard de Chardin and philosophers of science in the contemporary world, global issues, women's rights, alternative medicine and energy, and matters to do with electronics, genetics and communications. Some of the meditations attempt to apply psychological insights to scripture passages, although it must be said again that this so-called global spirituality mode can equally be seen as an adventurous and forward-looking contemporary Christian mode.

And yet, lying behind these eight, sometimes innovatory, modes there is a basic Protestant spirituality – indeed a spirituality involving Christians generally – that sees Christian prayer and spirituality as praising and thanking God. We see ourselves as flawed people needing and receiving forgiveness; we see that under God there are no limits to the perfect love that we can achieve; and we recognise that we can pray for ourselves and for others, accepting the responsibility that prayer involves action for others. We recognise that daily personal prayer, as a trigger to the total prayer of our lives, is crucial – for ourselves, for the church and for the world.

Acknowledgements

My thanks are due to a number of people, many of them unknown to the wider world, who have been of significant help to me on my spiritual pilgrimage and who have contributed, sometimes unwittingly, to the writing of these daily prayers. The seminal books on personal prayer by John Baillie, *A Diary of Private Prayer*, and Leslie Weatherhead, *A House of Prayer*, should also be mentioned.

In my home town of Pontefract in Yorkshire, where I came into contact with the church as a teenager through the sporting facilities of a Methodist Youth Club, the transparent spirituality of the Reverend Alfred Beardsley, the spiritual care of layfolk such as the McCarthy family, and the authentic devotion of various lay preachers were important. So too was the reminder from leaders of the day such as Donald Soper and W. E. Sangster that prayer and spirituality are the prerogative not of any particular church but of the whole Christian tradition.

As a student at Cambridge, the liturgy of Christ's College Chapel, the daily prayers at Wesley House, the weekly prayers of students from around the university and the warm fellowship of the Methodist Society Groups proved to be deeply significant.

As a young minister in Birmingham, contact with the natural devotion of industrial Brummies, especially that of Lilian Cowell, who led an extraordinary yet unselfconscious life of service and saintliness, was of real significance. So too was the simple and spontaneous spirituality of West Indians who were arriving in Britain at the time.

India gave me a rich experience of the spirituality of other religious traditions and of dialogue with them. A single day could begin with a Hindi lesson from a wonderful Hindu Pundit, Ambika Datta Upadhyaya, which would spill over into talk about prayer and spirituality, followed by a conversation with Stanley Hermit, the saintly Christian head of the college where I was manager, followed by a dialogue with a Hindu, a Muslim or a Buddhist at a deep level, followed by a visit to a Dom Muhallah where the sweepers of Banaras lived. A simple, wise, kindly Christian Dom named Pyare Lal, who was very lowly in Indian terms, became perhaps one of the deepest influences upon my life. So too did a Hindu holy man, Ram Kumar Singh, who came to 'find out about the Lord Christ' and eventually asked for baptism, becoming Paul Kumar Das.

He casually mentioned one day that he spent four hours each morning in deep meditation, and I learnt a great deal from him.

Back in Eastbourne, contact with lay families such as the Syruses and Greens, and ministers such as Douglas Thompson, was helpful. When invited to Harvard to do a doctorate, I found myself with fellow students from various cultures and religious traditions, and through the initiative of the deeply spiritual Professor Raimundo Panikkar we met together in the early morning before classes in a time of shared silence. Although the academic pace at Harvard was hectic, this made sure that the study of religion and the practice of religion were not divorced.

In Edinburgh from 1973 onwards, I am indebted to many people. Students at New College have been supportive not only in Spirituality and other courses but in countless other ways, as have different colleagues from John McIntyre and Tom Torrance onwards. Church of Scotland friends have welcomed me into their fellowship and given to me and received from me, as have Roman Catholics, such as Isobel Smyth, who have combined an inward spirituality associated with an Order with concerned practical involvement in the world. I am also indebted to colleagues in Religious Education circles in Britain, such as John Langdon, Douglas Scrimgeour, Peggy Morgan, Mary Hayward and Paul Williams, who combine precept and practice; great publishers, editors and writers on spirituality, including Richard Payne, Ewert Cousins, Seyyed Hossein Nasr and Wei Ming Tu; friends from other churches and other religious traditions who have guided me and prayed with and for me; and the members of my House Group in the Methodist Church with whom I can share anything in the confidence of spirituality. These people and groups, together with many others too numerous to be named, have shared my spiritual odyssey and helped directly or indirectly in the writing of this work. I hope this book can give back to others what I have received so richly. It is my original creation, and therefore its imperfections are mine; and yet, in writing it, I gladly own that I stand on the shoulders of so many others who to me are giants.

Finally, I thank Saint Andrew Press, and especially Ann Crawford, Richard Allen and Ann Vinnicombe, for their kind and careful work in seeing this book into print.

Scripture quotations are taken from the Holy Bible, New International Verson (NIV), copyright 1973, 1978, 1984 by the International Bible Society, used by permission of Hodder & Stoughton Ltd. Grateful thanks are due to the following for permission to use the indicated passages: the Society of Authors for copyright permission to use Sonnet XLIV and three passages from John Masefield, 'The Everlasting Mercy'; the Paulist Press for copyright permission to use two passages from Morton Kelsey, *Caring* (1981), and for copyright permission to use passages from the *Classics of Western Spirituality* volumes by St Bonaventure, George Herbert, Julian of Norwich, John and Charles Wesley, and Francis and Clare; Stainer & Bell Ltd for copyright permission to use Hymn 347 by Ian Fraser from *Hymns and Psalms*, and Hymn 412 by Fred Kaan from *Hymns and Psalms;* Mrs W. T. Davies for copyright permission to use Hymn 54 in *Hymns and Psalms* with an alternative verse by Rupert E. Davies; the estate of Helen MacNicol for copyright permission to use Hymn 539 in *Hymns and Psalms* translated by Nicol MacNicol; Cambridge University Press for copyright permission to use a passage from Aristides in *The Apology of Aristides* (1983); Continuum for copyright permission to use a prayer of D. T. Niles and a prayer of Charles de Foucauld from Geoffrey Chapman, *Unity Book of Prayers* (1969); the Methodist Publishing House for copyright permission to use three passages from Francis B. James, *For the Quiet Hour* (Epworth Press, 1952); Random House Group Ltd for copyright permission to use Laurence Housman, 'Love the Tempter' and 'A Prayer for the Healing of the Wounds of Christ'; HarperCollins Publishers for copyright permission to use two prayers from A. J. Arberry, *Sufism* (Allen & Unwin, 1950); Macmillan Publishers Ltd for copyright permission to use passages from N. Myers (ed.), *The Gaia Atlas of Planet Management* (1985); Faber & Faber Ltd for copyright permission to use a passage from Dag Hammarskjold, *Markings* (1964) and a passage from T. S. Eliot, *Murder in the Cathedral* (1968); the Methodist Publishing House for permission to use a number of hymns from *Hymns and Psalms*; Methuen Publishing Ltd for permission to use a piece from Julian of Norwich published in 1927; B. T. Batsford Ltd for permission to use passages by Donne and Wordsworth from *The Batsford Book of Religious Verse*; the Orion Publishing Group Ltd for permission to use passages by H. Coleridge, S. T. Coleridge, Taylor and Whittier from *English Religious Verse* (Dent) and for permission to use passages by Abu Bakr, Augustine, Channing, Dostoievsky, Hebrew prayer and Suso from *God of a Hundred Names* (Gollancz); Lion Publishing plc for permission to use two passages by Loyola and à Kempis from the Lion Handbook *History of Christianity*; Oxford University Press for permission to use passages by Dowden, Earle, Fletcher, Holmes, Rossetti and Thompson from *The Oxford Book of Mystical Verse* (Clarendon, 1921); and to Pearson plc for permission to use a passage from William James, *The Varieties of Religious Experience* (Longman, 1911).

Introduction

THE THEORY AND PRACTICE OF PRAYER

The heart of this book lies in the daily sets of prayers lasting for a month that are set out in the second part of the work. The reader is invited to share deeply in those prayers and, on the basis of this sharing, to follow his or her own path of prayer in a more significant and ordered way.

For those who wish to postpone using the actual prayers until the pages upon which they are written are reached, there is first of all a consideration of the theory of prayer lying behind the practice found in the second half of this book. The basic aim is that the reader should be motivated to set up his or her own method of prayer. If that method follows the one found in these pages, or goes beyond it, or even repudiates it, all well and good! It is vital for the individual person, for the Christian tradition and for the globe on which we live that prayer should become more effective. To that end this book is offered and shared.

For we live in the best of worlds and the worst of worlds. We live in a world of promise and a world of despair. We live on a planet of hope and a planet of blight. We live on an earth that can destroy itself or renew itself. We live at a time when the individual is freer and at the same time more in chains. We are alive at a time of aggressive materialism that is yet seeking to find the fruits of the inner world. We are threatened by spiritual malaise and we are beckoned by spiritual renewal. The evidence of rapid change is all around us. How can we live creatively in this bewildering, extraordinary, changing world? How can we understand it, change it, and gain a vision of its future? How can we understand better our own life, change our own life, and gain a vision of its future? If prayer means anything at all, it has to do with these basic questions, and it has to do with the God lying behind them. Prayer is central to creative living at the beginning of a new millennium.

HOW THIS BOOK CAME TO BE WRITTEN

How then did this book come to be written? For my previous books were in the main academic books commissioned by publishers in order to increase knowledge in the field of Religious Studies and Theology. I enjoyed writing them but there was an element of duty as well as privilege in finishing them. When deadlines beckoned, out came the typewriter and the work was completed.

This book was written out of a sense of inner compulsion. I felt a need to deepen my own prayer life. There was the challenge to grapple with prayer, to tap its laws, to understand its elements, to explore myself and God and my fellow creatures and the world in which we live.

John Wesley once commented, 'Preach faith until you have it, then when you have it you will preach faith.'[1] For me the motivation was 'explore prayer until you have it, then when you have it you will explore prayer'. This exploration included writing prayers, composing prayer-poems, and conceiving meditations as well as – or as part of – actual praying. Some of these prayers, poems and meditations are included in these pages.

However, the question remains, why publish a book on prayer? Apart from the obvious answers that writing is a natural form of expression and that one feels there is something very important that has to be said, the main reason is that I have a strong suspicion that I am everyman and everywoman as far as this matter of prayer is concerned. One suspects that there are millions of Christians in this world who would like to pray, or who would like to pray better, but they just do not know how to go about it. No one has ever taught them how to pray and they are not sure where to go for help. Like me, they have stopped and started, they have tried different approaches, but they have never 'cracked it'. They have been tempted to give up, or perhaps they have given up. They are living lives of quiet desperation, outwardly jovial but inwardly shallow. The unheard cry wells up within them, 'If only I really knew how to pray.' It is to meet this common need that these pages have been written. In writing for oneself one is writing for everyman and everywoman, and in writing for everyman and everywoman one is writing for oneself.

PERSONAL EXPERIENCE

Nowhere else in my writings have I written in such directly personal terms. My other books have been couched in terms of scholarship and have contributed to the ongoing process of building up academic knowledge. Nor is this book devoid of such knowledge. However, if there is any truth in the notion that my own experience of prayer and experiments with prayer mirror, in one way or another, those of many other people, it is only fair that I indicate my own gropings and struggles in order to be of existential as well as intellectual help to others.

Early Life and Entry into Christian Ministry

I was baptised Church of England but did not belong to a church-going family and was outside the orbit of the church until my early teens when the attractions of football, cricket and table tennis lured me into a Methodist Youth Club.

Even in those early years there was an occasional sense of there being 'something else' not confined to this world of matter and the senses. This 'something else' had no particular name but there was a sense that, whatever it was, it would respond in some way in time of need. In other words there was an incipient sense of prayer. It was part of my life and part of my human equipment, even though at that time I had no contact with the church.

Much later I came to know Sir Alister Hardy and I became acquainted with his Religious Experience Research Unit at Oxford. His words resonate with my experience:

> At certain times in their lives many people have had specific, deeply felt, transcendental experiences which have made them all aware of the presence of this power. The experience when it comes has always been quite different from any other type of experience they have ever had. They do not necessarily call it a religious feeling, nor does it occur only to those who belong to an institutional religion or who indulge in corporate acts of worship. It often occurs to children, to atheists and agnostics, and it usually induces in the person concerned a conviction that the everyday world is not the whole of reality: that there is another dimension to life.[2]

Prayer, then, or at any rate capacity for prayer, was quite simply part of human nature; it was part of being human. The sad thing was that for me, as for many others, it long remained a capacity rather than a discipline and a reality.

Eventually I became a Methodist minister and went for ministerial training to Wesley House, Cambridge. Here budding ministers received training in theology, preaching and praying in public. However, there was no training in private prayer. It was assumed that such prayer happened, but it was a personal matter. It was something you worked out, or didn't work out, for yourself.

The same thinking applied to the prayer life of laypersons. Like ministers, they too were assumed to have an instinctive knowledge of how to pray. Because ministers were not trained in spirituality, it was not likely that they would normally extend such training to layfolk. Training in prayer went by default. Lives with a deep commitment to prayer were by no means absent but they tended to be the exception rather than the rule.

Things have changed since the early 1960s. Protestant circles have begun to pay more serious attention to prayer and teaching about prayer. Paradoxically, Roman Catholic circles, after revelling in the freedom from regimented patterns of prayer afforded by Vatican II, are beginning to wonder whether that freedom is perhaps too great and are experimenting with middle ways between the old inflexibility and the new licence. Nevertheless, in different circles and for different reasons, there remains the sense that there is a need for more encouragement in prayer and for more guidance in prayer.

Reasons for Reluctance to Pray

Before continuing, it is worthwhile to pause for a moment and consider possible reasons for this reluctance to give prayer the attention it deserves. Seven such reasons have brought themselves to my attention during my wrestlings and it may be helpful to look at them now.

1   Ignorance about Prayer

The first we have glanced at already, namely a genuine ignorance about how to pray and a general absence of guidelines. Where do we pray? How do we sit, or stand, or kneel, or lie? How do we start? What do we do with our body? What are the steps in prayer? How long should it last? Do we speak or are we quiet? How do we visualise God? How do we visualise ourselves? What can we pray for? Who should we pray for? How do we end? Should we concentrate upon praising God or praying for others? What do we do with wandering thoughts? Should we use our imagination or avoid it? The questions are legion, and they can sometimes be so insistent or complex or plentiful that they inhibit the call to pray.

2   Busy Nature of Modern Life

In the second place there is the busy nature of modern life. There is family life, there is school, there is work, there are neighbours to help, there are causes to espouse. Prayer is a nice idea, but where do we find the time for it? It can so easily become navel-gazing that takes us away from the active concerns of the present age. It is an extra added on to our life. A welcomed extra, but still an extra. It is helpful to pray occasionally for the things and the people that lie directly on our minds. It is another string to our bow in helping them. But the point lies in the help and the activism, and prayer is secondary to them. It is an extra, and it is easy for it to become an optional extra. Many laypersons admit to the truth of this analysis, and so also do many ministers for whom hectic busy-ness becomes an occupational hazard.

3   Challenge of Prayer

A third reason for a reluctance to pray is a shrewd awareness of the dangers that might arise from taking prayer seriously. It is not an easy thing to fall into the arms of a loving God. It is not an easy thing to look at ourselves as we really are. We might have to change. Some of our old habits and attitudes might have to go. Prayer might offer abundant promise, but it also offers a threat to our cosy view of who we are and of our place in the scheme of things. If we take God seriously, as we may have to do if we take prayer seriously, the consequences are incalculable. If we examine ourselves in God's presence, promise to accept forgiveness and to forgive others, and open up the secrets of our inner world, what are we letting ourselves in for? There is an element of danger as well as glorious renewal in the whole enterprise.

4 *Confusion about Different Kinds of Prayer*

In the fourth place, it is easy to become confused about the different elements of prayer. One voice suggests to us that the point of prayer is to praise God and glorify him forever. Prayer is to do with God and not with ourselves. It is to praise him for his sake, not for what we can get out of it. Another voice suggests that prayer has to do with ourselves in relation to God. As we look at our lives there is much to be thankful for. Let us therefore review the blessings of our lives in all their detail and thank God for them. As we look at our lives there is also much to be sorry for. Let us therefore review the failings of our lives in all their detail and ask God's forgiveness and help in relation to those failings. Another voice suggests to us that prayer is to do with the opening up of our own inner world. As well as the outward world in which we live, there is a spiritual world that lies within us. The kingdom of God is within us. The opening up of that kingdom should be a major part of our concern, so our emphasis should be upon meditation and contemplation. Yet another voice suggests that prayer should not be individualistic but should concentrate upon other people. Did not Jesus, in the Lord's Prayer, stress our daily bread, our trespasses and our temptations? If the communion of saints is real, is it possible for us ever to pray on our own? Another voice suggests, alright, we should be aware of others and pray for others, but which others should we pray for? For those near at hand or the refugees, the starving, the dispossessed? Should we concentrate upon particular needs of particular local persons or raise our vistas to the problems of nuclear threat, ecological disaster, racial discrimination, injustice and oppression? Are these elements of prayer in opposition to one another, and if not which are most important? In adjudicating the matter, there is scope for emphasising one aspect of prayer at the expense of others and there is even scope for avoiding prayer at all.

5 *Intellectual Climate against Prayer*

A fifth reason for according a low priority to prayer lies in the intellectual climate in which the western world has lived and moved and had its being until recently. Whether we like it or not, we are subtly influenced by our education and background. Until recently the underlying world-view behind our educational system has stressed that the only real world is the external world of matter. We have access to that world through our senses and through reason. Our senses and our reason provide the avenue to truth. Modern science and technology have given impressive backing to their own world-view in the form of modern miracles, such as skyscrapers that soar upwards, spacecraft that take human beings to the moon, medicines that cure disease, material goods that increase outward prosperity. Only now are we beginning to realise the snags implicit in modern science, and only now are we beginning to realise that by its very nature it can only show us part of the world and tell us part of the truth. As youngsters and growing adults we were not to know this. When the prevailing educational world-view raised problems about a transcendent God over and beyond the outer world, some honest souls drew back from a deep involvement in prayer for intellectual reasons.

6   Reticence about Prayer

In the sixth place, a laudable but perhaps exaggerated regard for the supposed private and spontaneous nature of true prayer raised dilemmas for some people, especially Protestants. John Wesley in his life of the saintly early Methodist Fletcher of Madeley found difficulties in describing Fletcher's prayer-experience, which everyone knew to be very deep, because Fletcher himself rarely mentioned it. As Wesley put it:

> The pious members of the Church of Rome make a conscience of concealing anything from their Directors, but disclose to them all the circumstances of their lives, and all the secrets of their hearts: Whereas very few of the Protestants disclose to others, even their most intimate friends, what passes between God and their own souls, at least not of set purpose.[3]

Among some Christians, and not only Protestants, this reticence remains to share with others what is holy, unique and known only between the soul and God. This reticence is understandable and in some senses admirable. It is also holding hostages to fortune because experiences shared are more likely to be retained, repeated and deepened than experiences that are not shared.

7   Prayer as an Excuse for Arrogance

Our final reason for not giving high priority to prayer lies at the other end of the scale from the one we have just mentioned. May not too organised a discipline of prayer lead to spiritual pride and arrogance, and place the emphasis upon self-effort and human endeavours rather than on the grace of God? May it not become a programme of self-advance and self-therapy rather than a gift that is given and a work of the Spirit? May it not represent our own selfish view of what is good for us rather than true spiritual openness and growth? The honest answer surely is that it can – but it need not and should not. As St Paul put it, 'Work out your own salvation with fear and trembling, it is God who works within you' (Philippians 2:12–13). The usual alternative to having a discipline of prayer is not having a discipline of prayer; it is to attempt nothing.

To summarise briefly, there is an element of truth in all these seven reasons, and at times in my life I have seen some appeal in each one of them. How is one to pray if one has not been taught? How is one to make time for prayer in the midst of a busy life? Prayer may involve radical change in one's life. There are many different elements of prayer that do not always fit easily together. Our intellectual climate has not been supportive of a deep prayer discipline. Spiritual individualism can be a problem. It is possible for a discipline of prayer to become self-willed and arrogant.

However, these seven reasons can also be turned upside down. If the desire for prayer is there, it is increasingly possible to find people and books to be of help. If life is too busy for prayer, then it is just too busy, for prayer is the ideal foundation for a busy life. The renewing change in life that comes from prayer is deeply to be welcomed. The different elements of prayer help one another and make it more relevant. Our intellectual climate is altering to make a discipline of prayer less opposed to the spirit of the age. The spiritual life of each person is unique and that is a good thing. Disciplines of prayer give greater scope for the love of God to do its work in every part of our lives.

The capacity for prayer is part of our human birthright. All that is needed is a desire to explore it more fully in order to love God, our fellows and ourselves more deeply. We will find that this desire amounts to a prompting of God.

Experience in India

As well as spending some years in the Methodist ministry in Britain, I also spent four years as a missionary in north India. Three of these years were spent in the Hindu holy city of Banaras. During that time, part of my work was to engage in dialogue with Hindus and followers of other religious traditions. This work was very rewarding and stimulating. I had received no training in world religions; my expertise in this area was to come later. Everything was new; each conversation was likely to bring forth new insights. It was an exciting time.

1   Experience of Dialogue

Two things quickly became clear. The process of dialogue, if it was to mean anything, would involve receiving as well as giving. There were gifts that Christians could receive from Hindus as well as gifts that Hindus could receive from Christians. In this process of giving and receiving the whole realm of prayer began to loom larger. I met a number of Hindu gurus and saints who were obviously holy and spiritual people. Some of them, like Anandamayima, were internationally known figures; others were only known locally, although some of them were equally impressive. It was self-evident that their experience of prayer, contemplation and spirituality was central and crucial.

2 *Experience as Guru to a Hindu*

One particular relationship was especially challenging as far as prayer was concerned. I was approached by a Hindu sadhu who desired to have instruction in the Christian way. I agreed, and, from his point of view, I became his guru. Insofar as I was the teacher and he was the student, this was not an unreasonable position. However, in the course of our many conversations he casually mentioned that he got up at 3am every morning and spent four hours in deep meditation. This, of course, was way beyond anything I had ever dreamt of as far as prayer was concerned. To be considered his guru was a humbling experience, and it remains so to this day. As far as spirituality was concerned it should have been the other way round. Christian ministerial training in the west had offered preparation in preaching, pastoral care, teaching and administration: it had given little inkling about how to be a spiritual leader and guru.

3 *Stimulus to Christian Prayer from the East*

It is not surprising that a number of westerners desiring a deeper training in spiritual discipline have since turned to the east for guidance and experimented with Zen, Yoga, Transcendental Meditation and other eastern ways. This stimulus from the east is a challenge to the Christian tradition to wake up from its spiritual slumber and rediscover its own spiritual treasures. It is a jolt to the church, especially in the west, to take the discipline of prayer seriously. As well as being jolted by the east, Christians can also learn from the east. In my own case I was stimulated by dialogue with Hindus to become a more concerned Christian. However, it had less effect upon my experience of prayer than it might have done. I determined to take prayer more seriously – but not yet!

Experience as a University Teacher

Eventually after taking a Harvard doctorate I moved over into university teaching. The round of lecturing, researching, writing and dealing with students came into play. My areas of expertise were wide, covering various aspects of Religious Studies. Much of my time was spent in grappling with the technical aspects of Religious Studies, Comparative

Religion and Theology. The emphasis was necessarily upon the intellectual side rather than the prayer side of religion.

However, five elements of my work did spill over, at any rate theoretically, into the realm of prayer, and it is worth pausing to consider them now. It is probable that the reader will recognise traces of these five elements in his or her own thinking about prayer and about religion in general.

1 What do we mean by Religion?

In the first place there was the basic question of what is a religion? What do we mean when we talk about a religious tradition? Various models tried to answer this point but they seemed to deal with it in a way that undervalued the whole area of prayer and inwardness. In my own model, outlined below, I attempted to redress the balance. Underlying each religious tradition is a notion, indeed a reality, of transcendence. In the Christian case it is God; in other religious traditions it is named in different ways. This reality is ineffable, and therefore difficult to pin down intellectually and difficult to experience fully. Nevertheless it is the ultimate point of reference. This transcendence makes itself available to human beings, to you and me, through a mediating focus. In the Christian case it is Christ; in other religious traditions the mediator is named in different ways. In other words, lying behind each religious tradition there is transcendent reality made available to persons on earth through a mediating focus – lying behind Christianity there is God in Christ.

Within each religious tradition there are eight elements bound up together. There is a religious community binding together the people who belong to the religion – in the Christian case the church in its various forms. There are rituals of one sort or another – in the Christian case the sacraments, the great festivals, and various forms of worship. There are ethics, ideas about the good life – in the Christian case the ideal of loving God, loving one's neighbour and loving one another as Christ has loved us. There is the element of social involvement in wider society – in the Christian case actively helping the sick, the poor, the ignorant and the distressed. There are certain beliefs about God, human beings and the universe – in the Christian case these have been summed up in elaborate theologies. There is a scripture, a specially set-aside book or books – in the Christian case the Bible. However, there are two other elements that are seldom stressed but which are very important indeed, and which have to be added to the six elements already mentioned. They are, first, aesthetics, the whole area of music, art and literature – in the Christian case seen in hymns, painting, sculpture, stained-glass windows, religious dance and Christian literature. And finally there is spirituality, the whole dimension of prayer and inwardness – in the Christian case seen in a succession of mighty spiritual classics of prayer.

Lying behind these eight elements that combine together to form a religious tradition, there is something else. Perhaps the nearest word to describe it is faith. It is that which holds these elements together, gives them meaning, and uses them to relate us to the God in Christ who lies behind them. The eight elements are channels; they are a means to an end; they are vehicles whereby human beings have access through faith to God in Christ.[4]

This model is an intellectual model put together for intellectual reasons. However, it has three interesting implications for the life of prayer. Its main stress is upon persons. Religion is above all personal. The emphasis is not upon religions as such; it is not upon Christianity or any other religion as such. For religions as such cannot do anything for anyone. The eight elements within a religion may be lifeless unless they are brought together and given life by personal faith. The eight elements within Christianity are the means by which persons are put into contact with God in Christ. Religion is primarily a personal relationship with God, and religions together with the eight elements within them are a means to that end.

Second, although all of the eight elements including prayer can become ends in themselves devoid of faith and of God, it is above all prayer which can stimulate a personal faith and breathe life into the other elements. Its very nature is personal and experiential. Although church membership, attending rituals, doing good, social involvement, right belief, reading the Bible and interest in church music can and sometimes do become substitutes for personal faith, it is less likely that this can happen to prayer. For its aim is to put us into personal contact with ultimate reality. A life of prayer is usually an excellent touchstone of the reality of personal faith.

The third implication of the model is that religious traditions can be seen as wholes. As far as the Christian tradition is concerned, the emphasis is not upon the Roman Catholic, or Anglican, or Methodist, or Orthodox, or any other particular branch of the Christian tradition. It is upon the tradition as a whole. The prayers in the second part of this work include jewels from every branch of the Christian tradition, and this book is designed to be of help to members of every part of the Christian community.

2 *The Wesleys*

An invitation to speak on the Wesleys at a summer school in Edinburgh involving American Methodists, and an invitation to be keynote speaker on the topic of the Wesleys at the Indiana School of the Prophets, led me to do research on the spirituality of the Wesleys, which resulted in my book on the Wesleys in the *Classics of Western Spirituality*. On the face of it, this involved delving back into the roots of one specific part of the Christian tradition. And in practice this is what happened. There was a period of research into the spiritual foundations of the success of the Wesleys, and into the beginnings of the Methodist tradition. The results were revealing. For lying behind the work of the Wesleys was a spirituality of quite unusual breadth and depth and catholicity.

The sources of their prayer life were wide. At the Epworth rectory, they were exposed by their parents, Samuel and Susannah Wesley, not only to the Bible and the Prayer Book but also to spiritual classics ranging from the Scot Henry Scougal's *The Life of God in the Soul of Man* and the work of the Roman Catholic Pascal to the accounts of their work by the Danish missionaries in Georgia. At Oxford, John Wesley was deeply influenced in 1725 by the Anglican Jeremy Taylor's *Rules and Exercises of Holy Living and Dying* to seek for purity of intention in all he did; and soon afterwards two books by another Anglican, William Law, *Christian Perfection* and *A Serious Call to a Devout and Holy Life*, showed him the futility of being half a Christian and persuaded him of the need to devote his whole life to God. Wesley was also influenced at Oxford by masters of Roman Catholic spirituality such as Thomas à Kempis, John of the Cross, Pascal, Scupoli, Quesnel, Fénelon, de Renty, Mme Bourignon, Mme Guyon, Tauler, Molinos and the Theologica Germanica, with their stress upon pure love and total resignation. In the Holy Club at Oxford the Wesleys also went back behind the spiritual classics of the western tradition, whether Protestant or Catholic, to writers of the eastern tradition such as Macarius the Egyptian, Clement of Alexandria, Ephraim Syrus and the Cappadocian Fathers. Their missionary experience in Georgia put the Wesleys into contact with the Moravians and the German Pietist tradition, which sparked off a series of events which led to John's famous Aldergate Street experience of 1738. When John Wesley published the fifty volumes of his *Christian Library* from 1750 to 1756 in order to help the early Methodist preachers, that *Library* was a wide-ranging selection of spiritual writings including most of the writers mentioned above. In short, the spiritual roots of the Wesleys lay in Orthodox and Roman Catholic as well as Lutheran, Moravian, Church of England and Puritan sources.[5]

In addition to this, the Wesleys also used many different kinds of prayer. As seen above, they used prayer arising out of reading spiritual classics. They were also fond of the Prayer Book and the sacraments. Liturgical and sacramental prayers were their constant companions. As is well known, they were not confined to set prayers, although they revered traditional formulations, and they were masters of extempore preaching and extempore prayer. Nor were they strangers to silent prayer, which often involved reflective meditation on the Bible or on spiritual classics. They also composed their own prayers in the form of written prayers and, just as importantly, the Wesleys – and above all

Charles Wesley – composed many famous hymns, some of which were, in effect, sung prayers. They covered the whole gamut of prayer. Their prayer forms were not simplistic or monolithic, they were rich and many sided.

However, although prayer was important to the Wesleys, it was not an end in itself. Their total spirituality was wider than their prayer life, and their prayer life fed into their total life which was aimed at perfect love for God and other humans. As far as they were concerned, although the prayer life of the individual was important, it was part of a greater whole. That greater whole included the fellowship and worship of the Christian community. John Wesley ranks as one of the greatest spiritual organisers in the history of the church, and the masterpiece of his system of connected spirituality was the small fellowship group. In his view, although prayer might be private, its fruits and implications were public. Nor were its public fruits confined to the fellowship of Christians. As he put it, the love of a Christian soars above narrow boundaries 'embracing neighbours and strangers, friends and enemies, yea, not only the good and gentle but also the froward, the evil and unthankful. For he loves every soul that God has made, every child of man, of whatever place or nation.'[6] Thus, in his day, Wesley was a great social reformer who built schools and wrote books for the education of the needy, visited prisons and went to the help of the poor, learnt that he could satisfy his own needs on £28 a year and was ready to dispose of the rest of his wealth, opposed corruption, whether it be in church or state, whose motto 'go to those who need you most' took him on horseback a quarter of a million miles, especially into areas of greatest need, and who was the first great Englishman to proclaim against slavery. Therefore a study of the spirituality of the Wesleys amply demonstrated that the forms and implications of prayer were very wide-ranging indeed.[7]

3 Classics of Spirituality

The third element in my work that fed into reflection on prayer established the point that the forms and implications of prayer could be more wide-ranging than even the Wesleys had anticipated in that they need not necessarily be confined to the Christian tradition. In recent years three great series of volumes on spirituality have been conceived and partly brought into being. We may note in passing that the fact that commercial presses have set out in confidence to publish not far short of 150 volumes on spirituality is a symbol of the growing interest in spirituality and prayer that is abroad in the world.

The first series was the *Classics of Western Spirituality*, in which my volume on the Wesleys appeared. The series was planned to come out in sixty volumes, beginning in 1978, and was extended by another ten volumes or so in view of its success. The writers covered are mainly Christian spiritual writers from the Catholic, Orthodox or Protestant traditions. However, the word 'western' is seen in its widest sense, and at least five volumes are devoted to the spirituality of each of the Jewish, Muslim and American-Indian traditions. In the process a treasure-house of prayer has been opened up in these traditions.

The second series is *World Spirituality: An Encyclopedic History of the Religious Quest*. This twenty-five volume enterprise aims to look at the historical development of the spiritual wisdom of humanity from early times until the present day. Through my involvement as a consultant, I have been able to follow the progress of the project, the first volume of which was published in 1985, and to see the depths of prayer and spirituality present in all the religious traditions of the world including Christianity.

The third series is the *Classics of Eastern Spirituality* to be published in sixty volumes. It will make available the major spiritual writings of the Buddhist, Hindu, Confucian, Taoist, Primal and other traditions of the east. In this way a further treasure-house of prayer will be forthcoming.[8]

The second part of this book concentrates on Christian prayer, and it is intended mainly for western Christians. It would be difficult to write a book that would be of practical and experiential help to western Christians that contained numerous examples of prayers from other religions. Nevertheless this work does contain a few prayers taken from other religions and also a few prayers taken from non-western Christian communities as a gesture and symbol of the fact that the time is going and has gone when non-Christian religions and non-western Christianity can be ignored in a book of Christian prayer.

4   The Emerging Global Situation

The fourth element of my work relevant to prayer relates to the global situation of our world. The last twenty years have witnessed a heightened awareness of both our global dilemma and our global possibilities. Through membership of the New York Center for Integrative Studies as well as through my work in Religious Studies I have become involved in an exploration of global issues. Prayer involves the desire and obligation to pray for the world. Many Christians feel prompted to pray for the world but find it hard to do so. Contemporary global problems seem too vast. The horrors of famine, poverty, malnutrition, nuclear threat, injustice, ecological disaster, population growth and human inhumanity seem too difficult to understand or to begin to understand. The temptation is to throw up one's hands in despair and say that prayer cannot cope with the complexity of these problems. The need is for a system of thought that can fit these problems into a framework of understanding that makes some sort of sense of them so that we can pray intelligently about them. The need is for hopeful prayer and for prayerful hope so that even the worst human nightmares to do with AIDS, nuclear destruction, mass starvation and the collapse of the earth itself can be contained within a positive rather than a negative spirituality.

Clearly in a short space it is possible to do no more than hint at ways of making the global situation amenable to creative prayer. It may be helpful to see the global situation at three levels. At one level there is the earth itself. When human beings first saw our planet from space they saw clouds, seas, forests, mountains and plains. The only human edifice remotely visible was the Great Wall of China. It became clear that the earth is one and that human beings depend upon that earth to feed them, keep them alive, and sustain them. It is not like a house that can be added to when a family grows larger. If species of animals are wiped out, if medicinal herbs in forests are annihilated, if jungles are cut down, if deserts grow, if energy sources are used up, if the ozone layer protecting the earth is punctured by polluting substances, if acid rain spreads, if the climate warms, if there are more Chernobyls and Bhopals and worse, there are consequences not only for the earth but for the human beings living on the earth. The fate of human beings is linked to the fate of the earth. Christian prayer has taken God and human beings seriously. It has not given sufficient attention to the earth itself. A new version of the earth as a providing force that is threatened but which can and must be saved and sustained is required of meaningful Christian prayer.

The second level is that of human beings. They, too, are ultimately one. There may be different races; they are part of the human race. There may be different nations; they are part of the totality of nations. There may be different ideologies; they are part of the overarching ideology of humanity. There may be different religions; they are part of the greater whole of humankind. When Christians pray in terms of 'we', the ultimate 'we' is not our family, our town, own nation, our religion – it is not we whites or blacks, we British, we westerners, we socialists or capitalists, we Christians – it is we human beings. The need for a new vision of understanding, peace and love between human beings is paramount. The need for a new vision of humanity is paramount. Prayer for particular people in particular situations remains important but it finds its place within a vision of the whole.[9]

The third level is that of God and the spiritual life. Whether we can say that God is ultimately one is a complex theological question. What we can say, most of us will agree, is that our view of God is too small. If God is anything, He/She/It is God of the whole world and of all the people in the world. Perhaps God as such is too ineffable to be fully known. Perhaps we ourselves are too ineffable fully to know ourselves! Our vision of who we are and of who God is grows. We can only pray with as much of ourselves as we know to as much of God as we know. Yet our vision of God is growing. So is our vision of the spiritual life. For we are a privileged people. We share the problems of an inter-dependent world, but we also share the resources of an inter-dependent world. And these resources include the spiritual resources of the globe. They also include insights from various sources into the inner world, the spiritual world, the psyche, and the kingdom of God, that are available, within human beings.[10]

5   *All Life is a Whole*

The fifth element in my work relevant to prayer is centred upon a growing sense of the inter-relationship between different levels of knowledge and different levels of consciousness. I discovered that the three levels mentioned above, the level of the earth, the level of human beings, and the level of God and the inner world, are not separate but related. Moreover the same is true of our individual consciousness. Our consciousness of our body, of our mind and of our spirit is not separate but related.

Western scholarship has gone in the direction of stressing separate subjects, separate disciplines, separate specialisations, and the analysis of particular problems in isolation from each other. Recently there has been a trend in the opposite direction. There has arisen a greater concern for the wholeness, integration and inter-connectedness of knowledge. The systems-view in science sees the world under the headings of integration and inter-relatedness. The Gaia view of nature popularised by Lovelock sees the whole earth as a living organism which is greater than the sum of its separate parts. Recent research into health and wholeness stresses the inter-relationship between body, mind and soul and the need to think in terms of the whole person as far as successful medicine is concerned. There is a greater readiness to link economics and ecology, so that if a factory is making fat profits while at the same time pouring pollution into the Firth of Forth the 'cost' of that pollution should be subtracted from the 'profits'. As E. F. Schumacher has argued, the crux of economic life – and life in general – is that it constantly requires the living reconciliation of opposites.[11] In another context we could spend many pages looking at the new seeds of integrative thought springing up in many different areas of knowledge. Things and people are inter-connected; that is the message. We are not solitary beings. Every creature is, in some sense, connected to and dependent on the rest. In the light of all this, prayer can be seen to be not only an isolated act carried out by you or I in separation from all else, it is inter-related with the whole of our life and has its effects on the whole of our life. It also reverberates out into the life of the world. No prayer, then, is an island aloof from all else. Prayer is part of a dynamic continuum involving ourselves, other human beings, God and nature.

Depth Psychology and C. J. Jung

My own thinking has been stimulated along these lines by some of the depth psychologists, especially by C. J. Jung, and we will end this section by considering his relevance for the life of prayer. He was quite clear about the inter-connectedness of God, human beings and the world, and he traced many of the problems of modern persons and the modern world to a lack of self-knowledge and a lack of experience of God.

1 Knowing God

Shortly before his death in 1961 Jung fielded a question by a BBC radio interviewer, John Freeman, about belief in God by saying that he did not need to believe: he knew. For him the root of religion was experience of God. In a famous statement he said, 'among all my patients in the second half of life – that is over thirty-five – there has not been one whose problem in the last resort was not that of finding a religious outlook on life'.[12] As far as Jung was concerned, this religious outlook need not necessarily be connected with a particular creed or membership of a church. It was a potentiality within human nature; it was a human birthright; it was an inherent possibility that could become real within all persons.

Clearly prayer is an effective way of opening up and making real the religious impulse that is already there in human beings. In working on Jung, while far from agreeing with everything that he said, I found a number of ideas that were relevant to prayer. Although the divisions of prayer into Approach, Praise, Thanks, Self-Examination and Forgiveness, Meditation, Petition, Intercession and Contemplation that occur in the second part of this book were worked out without reference to Jung, his work appeared to be very relevant to those different aspects of prayer.

2 Praise of God

Jung speaks of a God-archetype that is latent in human beings and waiting to be aroused. There is a God instinct within our very self and God is already with us waiting to be discovered. It is not a question of drawing down a distant God by our will and efforts; it is a question of uncovering or 'knowing' the God who is already within. The prayer of praise or adoration is a good way of doing this. It is to give honour to the God who is deeply immanent within us as well as around and beyond us. It is to open up the kingdom of God that is within us as well as around and beyond us.

3 God Instinct and Thanking God

Jung also speaks of forces within us that move us in the direction of health and wholeness. There are forces that lead us in the direction of growth and change. These forces are sometimes held back by traumas of childhood rejection, societal neglect, personal tragedy or deep anguish that are repressed into our unconscious mind and block our growth. They succeed in fixing us in the past and cutting us off from the present. Nevertheless they cannot obliterate the God instinct within us; they can only veil it. For Jung the antidote is to understand ourselves under God and to live in the present. In cases of severe blockage, professional or other therapy may be required to make this possible. However, the basic aim is that we should be in creative balance with our selves, with our environment and with God, who is both caring and responsive. The basic reality with which we have to concern ourselves is growing and caring and being responsive. The attitude of prayer to which this corresponds is that of thanksgiving. Nothing can separate us from the love of God.

4 Forgiveness

This does not mean that Jung undervalues evil and what he calls the 'shadow' side within human beings. He argues that we are often unaware of the evil and the shadow side within us, and we are often unaware, too, of the masculine side within us if we are female and the feminine side within us if we are male. We not only fail outwardly; the roots of our failure are deep-seated – they are unconscious and they lie within us. We know only part of ourselves, and, in order to shield ourselves from our failings, we justify ourselves or we blame others. We find it hard truly to examine ourselves because this requires that we know ourselves and see ourselves as we really are, and this is often hard to bear. Prayer relates this syndrome to the whole question of forgiveness. We are forgiven by God and therefore we can forgive ourselves. We forgive others and therefore we are free. As Jung put it, 'if only people could realise what an enrichment it is to find one's own guilt, what a sense of humour and spiritual dignity!'[13]

5 Prayerful Imagination and Meditation

In order to know ourselves, Jung advocates various means among which is the exercise of active imagination. This can be exercised on dreams, in sharing with friends, in painting, in reflecting on images and symbols, and in meditation. It opens up our inner world and helps us better to understand ourselves, others and God. As part of the meditations used in this book, some focus upon various sorts of active imagination. By taking a biblical story, for example, we can, by use of the active imagination, pass over into Joseph or Jacob, share the sandals of the disciples on the road to Emmaus, be with Jesus in the Garden of Gethsemane. We can retreat into the inner room of our soul and commune with the living God.

6 Asking God for Things

Jung also refers to the child archetype within the human personality, that part of us which makes it natural to ask for things and to trust in another.

He also suggests that there are powerful resources deep within us and available to us that can help us to solve dilemmas and to crack problems. Within this context petitionary prayer becomes natural. It is not a question of forcing or persuading God but of opening up and committing our inner resources so that, in 'becoming as little children', we become adult channels through whom prayer can flow.

7 *Intercession*

Jung's theory of the universal unconscious suggests that we all have access to a basic reservoir of symbols and inter-connections, which, although hidden, are real. We saw earlier how some developments within modern science corroborate the notion of interdependence. Telepathy is another area that suggests that contact between people can leap over boundaries of space. Within this realm of ideas it becomes more credible to think of intercessory prayer for others as being meaningful, not just in terms of what it does for the one who prays but also in terms of what is done for the recipient of prayer. Jung's psychological theories become relevant to the whole drama of intercession.

During the last few pages I have indicated five elements in my academic work that have spilled over into the realm of prayer. However, there was no necessary reason why work that impinged upon the theory of prayer should be carried over into the practice of prayer. Indeed, there were some reasons why it might be argued that it should not. After all, studies of models of religion, studies of the spirituality of the Wesleys, studies of the classics of western and eastern spirituality, studies of global issues, and studies of integration between fields of knowledge pursued by people such as Jung remain studies. They belong to the field of scholarship. They can be pursued, in principle, by atheists and agnostics who have no intention or desire to translate theories into practice. And it is right and proper that this should be the case. It is possible for subjective religious experiences to vitiate the process of scholarship in religion by introducing distortion and bias into a field that can do without them. Indeed, in my own work on the methodology of Religious Studies, I was at pains to make the case for Religious Studies as an exciting and developing new field of study on academic grounds.[14] It is of paramount importance that scholarship in the field of the study of religion should be of the highest academic standard. However, to jump from the need for excellence and freedom from bias in the study of religion to the notion that there should be no connection between theories of religion and the practice of religion is too big a leap to make, especially as far as prayer is concerned. Although theories about prayer and the practice of prayer are separable in principle, it would be strange if there were no link between them.

Indeed at another level the opposite view may apply. It is possible to theorise about prayer, and read books about prayer, and to go to talks about prayer, but not to get round to the actual business of praying. Intellectualising about prayer may get in the way of praying. In the experience of the author and, I imagine, the readers, both temptations are possible: to judge theories of prayer and scholarship about prayer by the standard of one's own subjective experience, and to suppose that there is no connection at all between the theory and practice of prayer. Both extremes militate against true prayer and true intellectual integrity.

Call to a Deeper Practice of Prayer

How then did I feel the need to enter more seriously into the practice of prayer? From one point of view it has always been the case that I have taken prayer seriously in the sense that I knew intuitively that it was very important. For much of the time it has remained, however, at a relatively superficial level. I suspect again that I am everyman and everywoman as far as this is concerned. We all knew in our hearts of hearts that prayer was of ultimate significance but we were not moved to give it the systematic discipline we knew it deserved.

1 Experiments

In my case five circumstances conspired together to open up within me a deeper order of prayer. In the first place I tried various different methods of praying. They were all of greater or lesser help but they were all useful in their own way. At one level there were the spasmodic encounters: 'Hi, Lord, how are you doing today?'; 'Be with our athletes at the Olympics'; 'So-and-so is in trouble, please help them, Lord'; 'Thank you for this gift, for this success'; and so on. At another level there were trial runs with orders of morning and evening prayer. In other words there were attempts to use liturgies on a daily basis. These worked for a time but sooner or later the motivation lessened, the practice decreased, and eventually it diminished into insignificance. Liturgical repetitions work for others; of that I am aware. But somehow they did not speak at a deep level to my need. Perhaps I remain an innate Protestant and yet I suspect that most Christians yearn inwardly for a prayer life that is theirs uniquely. In fact the liturgies of the Christian tradition remain important to me on a weekly basis, but I find they need to be complemented by something else. At a third level various books of prayer came into play. One by one, at different times, sundry collections of prayers have spoken to my need. John Baillie's *A Diary of Private Prayer*, D. H. Southgate's *Draw Near to God*, Michael Quoist's *Prayers of Life*, Leslie Weatherhead's *A Private House of Prayer*,

W. E. Orchard's *The Temple*, and (more recently) various of the *Classics of Western Spirituality* have been of significant help.[15] All these three methods of praying – extempore, liturgical and reading spiritual classics – pointed in the direction of the need for a deeper systematic discipline. They not only pointed out the direction, they also fed into that eventual discipline.

2 Prayer and Life Connected

In the second place, there was a growing awareness that prayer and living were intimately related. In order to live it was necessary to pray, and in order to pray it was necessary to live. As one looked back, there was the dawning realisation that prayer was the basic reason why I had become intimately involved with the Christian church. The desire to practise the presence of God, the desire to be spiritually related with the divine for the living of life, had been primary motivations for taking the Christian tradition seriously. Yet somehow the point of it all, the crux of the matter, had been relegated to a secondary place. More attention had been given to the organising of the Christian community, to the rituals of the church, to ethical and social matters, to aesthetic considerations, and to scripture and theology. I was reminded of some words of a colleague and friend, J. L. Mehta, who died recently:

> Not until living itself is transformed into a pilgrimage, which is nothing if not living in the face of death, one's own, does Scripture disclose its sovereign majesty, become truly Scripture. We scholars play around with words, study them, manoeuvre them, and torture them, do things to them. But our pilgrimage through words is no pilgrimage until words begin to do things to us and to become the Word by which we live.[16]

Fellow scholars will recognise the truth of this statement but so, one suspects, will fellow Christians. It is easy to live and act at a superficial level of words and outward things. The answer seems to be to ground words and acts in prayer.

3 A Spiritual Director

In the third place, a Spiritual Director came into my life. For a period of two or three years I went every month to talk and share with a local Episcopalian minister on a no-holds-barred basis as far as my prayer life and my general life were concerned. This was a new and liberating experience. Secret things were shared and they stopped being secret. It was possible to talk in depth about the spiritual life, and it soon became clear that talking about prayer must spill over into talking about every part of life. Moreover, talking about prayer and praying must go hand-in-hand. It is no surprise that spiritual direction is becoming more common in many parts of the Christian community at this time. It is a symbol of the desire for greater depth in the life of prayer.

4 *Raja-yoga*

In the fourth place, there was an increasing motivation towards prayer resulting from some of the projects I was involved in. My research into the Raja-yoga movement brought me into contact with their British branches in Edinburgh and London, and it also took me to their headquarters at Mount Abu in Rajasthan. Their spirituality turned out to be impressive. It was both deep and specific. Part of my problem with Christian prayer had been its vagueness in both theory and method. Who do we pray to? Is it God the Father, Jesus Christ, the Trinity, or what? What are the stages in prayer? Do we start with God, with ourselves, with others? What are the parts played by intellect, emotion and will in prayer? What do we actually do when we pray? How do we localise God when we pray to him? It transpired that the basis of prayer in the Raja-yoga movement was to spend 45 minutes in deep meditation from 4 am to 4.45 am. This period was divided into three sections. The first focused upon the question, who am I? And the answer was that I am a soul, a child of God. The second centred upon God himself and its basic feature was direct conversation with God. The third switched the attention to other people and was engaged in sending out prayer vibrations on behalf of others. It seemed desirable to transpose the clarity if not the specific content of Raja-yoga prayer into a Christian framework. The same principle of creative borrowing from other traditions applied to other experiences. For example, involvement in the opening ceremonies of the Samye Ling Tibetan Buddhist temple at Eskdalemuir in the Scottish Borders through chairing an inter-faith symposium gave intimate contact with a different tradition of prayer which could also be adapted into the Christian tradition. In any case sharing prayer with others was a stimulus to setting up a more creative discipline of Christian prayer.[17]

5 *Challenge of the World*

Finally, outward events supervened as well. At one level there had come the ability to think globally, to put world events into some sort of order that made sense of them, to hang them on pegs that gave them a framework of meaning. Even so there was a growing feeling of impotence at the enormity of certain tragedies. During the period of a few years there came news of the flooding of the Nile at Khartoum and the emergence of a catastrophic famine in the Sudan; news came of similar flooding in Bangladesh whereby 20 million people effectively lost their homes; later hurricanes swept through the Caribbean and wrecked Jamaica and parts of Mexico and eastern USA. Reason and the facility to put these events into a framework of understanding were not enough. There arose a sense of rage that was also a sense of prayer. One could empathise with Job when he cried out, 'I am not at ease, neither am I quiet, neither have I rest.'[18] The need was not so much to put these events into a framework of thought where one could make sense of them (although that was not unimportant) but rather to put them into a framework of prayer where one could become involved in them. They were part of the framework of God in that they were part of the pain of God. As Teilhard de Chardin put it:

> By means of all created things, without exception, the divine assails us, permeates us, moulds us. We imagined it as distant and inaccessible, whereas in fact we live steeped in its burning layers.[19]

At the same time one was aware that it was no good making the burning layers of the divine, or dis-ease, or disquiet, or unrest the basis for prayer. They are the probes towards active compassion in prayer but undergirding them is a divine understanding and wisdom. Equally it was no good basing one's own prayer for the world upon one's inner rage against the planet's iniquities, or upon one's own dis-ease, or disquiet, or unrest – important as they were. Undergirding them was the fact of having coped bravely with one's own world and having had courageous converse with one's own inner problems. Prayer for the world was an extension of and a development of personal striving rather than an escape from it. Yet it must be an activity of prayer. The realisation arose that the best way of helping the world was to pray for it, and that this kind of prayer was likely to be exciting and difficult.

And so it was a combination of the five circumstances outlined above that led me into a deeper systematic discipline of prayer that lies behind this book. Yet all the time there was also a sense that it was not so much my discipline of prayer as that of God working within me. It was not so much me finding God as God finding me. And because this was the case there was also a sense that this was not just a private unfolding but something of universal interest. There was a sense in which my journey was the journey of everyman and everywoman. There was the conviction that by making this book available to all many people would be called to use it, and in using it to go beyond it, to the end that the force of prayer might be deepened in themselves and in the world.

How to Use this Book

In this final section I will set out three different ways of using this book. It is difficult to generalise because you who are reading the book now are different kinds of people. Some are men, some are women; some are young, some are not so young; some are married, some are not married; some are working, some are not working; some are black or white or brown or yellow or red; some are British and European, some are from other continents; some are Methodist, or Catholic, or Presbyterian, or Orthodox, or Episcopalian, or from other churches; some are agnostic, or belong to other religions; some are searching, some have found; some are happy, some are pensive. Whoever you are, and whatever your condition, I hope that this book of prayer can speak to your need. In order to help, let me point out three different ways into prayer through using this book.

Before embarking upon the three ways – which require little time, more time, and a lot of time – it is important first of all to prepare to pray. This may not always be possible. A friend of mine claimed that he was so busy that the only time he could find to pray was when he was shaving! Another friend argued that her busy schedule meant that the best time to pray was on the bus going to work in the middle of the city! Even so – if the book is planted next to the shaving mirror or taken on the bus – it is helpful to pause for a while and to be still so that we can remember who we are and that God is God. As we shall see if there is more time it is highly desirable to prepare more thoroughly; but as a minimum there should be a short and deliberate pause for reflection and concentration.

The First Way

The first and least demanding, and perhaps therefore the least rewarding, way is to read the prayers of each day straight through. This can be done fairly quickly. It can even be repeated later in the day.

Insofar as the whole gamut of prayer is covered each day, the exercise can be a rewarding one.[20] Albeit in quick compass, there is the chance to read an evocative sentence, to praise God, to give thanks for one's blessings, to contemplate one's own shortcomings and offer them up, to reflect upon a short meditation, to pray for oneself, to offer concern for others, and to take along the journey of the day a closing thought that can be returned to as need arises.

Benefit can certainly be obtained from using the book in this way. It is possible, however, that it may become an exercise in reading rather than an exercise in praying. As such it can be helpful, especially if it is part of a total concerned life. And yet more is possible.

The Second Way

The second way requires more time and more discipline. Ideally it requires a particular time and place each day so that a pattern of prayer can be established. This may not always be possible in a large family, or in a semi-detached Wimpey, or in circumstances of constant change. But insofar as it is attainable, it can be very helpful. The time and the place are not important in themselves, nor is the book important in itself. They are means to the end of practising the presence of God, setting up a discipline of prayer, and being of more help to others. And yet without the means, the end can sometimes become more difficult.

For most people a comfortable chair in a quiet place is desirable. This allows the body to be relaxed and the mind to be still. Consciously stilling the body by relaxing each part of it in turn can help.[21] So also can controlling and watching the breathing be of assistance in preparing one to pray.[22]

God is there anyway. But we can only approach as much of God as we know with as much of ourselves as we know. And stilling ourselves so that we can be open to God is a rewarding part of preparation.

The opening sentence of each day's prayer can be a significant element in 'getting ready'. A phrase such as 'Be still and know that I am God' and the other opening sentences prepare the heart and still the mind. It is often helpful to repeat the phrase in the silence of the heart so that the sense of being still and of knowing the presence of God increases within one's being.

Then each section of the day's prayers may be reflected on in turn. In addition to the general approach to God and recognition of God one can offer one's own approach and recognition; further to general thanks one can offer one's own thanks; beyond general admission of shortcomings one can offer one's personal admission of shortcomings; over and above reading the meditation one can reflect upon it personally; as well as saying general prayers for oneself and for others, one can add more personal prayers for oneself and others. One can look forward to the potential events of the day or look back on the actual events of the receding day in the light of the written prayers. And finally one can take the closing sentence as a talisman for hope, reflection and renewal within the total life of the day in question.

The second way requires more time than the first. It can be pursued without great eating into schedules. It takes with it the possibility of influencing schedules insofar as there is the intention to integrate spirituality into the whole of life.

The Third Way

By having available and making available more time, the third way takes deeper the process and discipline that have already been opened up in the first and second ways. Above all it aims to deepen the interior life for the sake of the world and to the glory of God.

Before looking at the third way in more detail let us first examine how it aims to take the process of prayer deeper. First, it sees reading the book as part of a total spirituality. It may combine the prayer involved in reading the book with other forms of prayer – liturgical, extempore, silent – but it will also see the reading of the book as helping and being helped by fellowship with others, and as aiding and being aided by a deeper involvement in the world. For the third way there is no such thing as a purely inward spirituality and no such thing as a purely solitary spirituality. Inward spirituality, fellowship with others, and involvement in the world are *all* important. All are part of a total spirituality. However, neither can a total spirituality do without inward spirituality as part of the full powerhouse that motivates periodic detachment from the world in order to be fully involved in the world.

Second, loving God, loving one's neighbour and loving oneself are all significant elements in a full spirituality. In the book all are stressed throughout. And they are stressed with a view to being lived. If we are to love our neighbours as ourselves we must first of all have a healthy regard for ourselves under God in order to love our neighbours. By the same token if we are to love the world today, that world must include the world of nature threatened by ecological abuse as well as the world of other persons threatened by other kinds of abuse.

Third, the third way involves the world of imagination. The training of the imagination is important, especially in our own day. Where does our mind wander when it is free? Within what gardens does it roam when it is not confined to customary paths? The opening and closing sentences in the book are intended as spurs to the imagination. The opening sentence is a haven for the mind to return to during the process of prayer; the closing sentence is a haven for the mind to return to after the process of prayer. Some of the meditations involve creative use of the imagination to fly back through time and space to be with Jesus or other figures at important times in their lives. They are aimed partly at creating healthy and creative grooves in the imagination.

In the fourth place, the third way emphasises personal growth including personal spiritual growth. The renewal of the personal life, outward and inward, is a significant part of total spirituality. However, it is not a matter of purely personal growth. As John Donne put it, no person is an island; as John Wesley put it, there is no such thing as a solitary Christian; as John Wesley also intimated, it is necessary to go not just to those who need us but to those who need us most.[23] Thus personal prayer is for personal involvement in the church and in the world as well as for personal delight in God and our own being.

And, fifth, the third way involves going beyond the systems of others in order to build up our own system. This book is of help to the extent that it is used and then transcended. It is a means to an end and not an end in itself – the end being the building up of our own discipline of prayer for the sake not only of ourselves but also of the church and of the world. By keeping a diary perhaps, by writing things down as we come across them, by remembering our dreams, by reading, by learning from our daily lives, by being aware and being involved – in so many ways we can nurture a creative spirituality that is akin to the fruits of the spirit.

The relevance of the book for the third way has been intimated in the points mentioned above: the use of the opening and closing sentences, the adoration of God, giving thanks for our own lives, using our imagination in the meditation, praying empathetically for ourselves and for others, concerned, and if necessary, sacrificial involvement in the lives of others, concern for the environment as well as people, inward growth for outward fruit, ongoing practice of the presence of God.

Suffice it to say that the first, second and third ways may overlap. If the third way presupposes more engagement of time and a greater seriousness this does not demean the first and second ways. Indeed, each reader will create his or her own way whether it be first, second, or third!

My fervent hope is that those who read this book will be enriched and encouraged to launch out into the depths of prayer in a way that has not been their experience before.

In the light of my own experience, and in the light of the needs of the church and the world as well as of ourselves, I can see no other deeper need at the present time. For what shall it profit a person if he or she gain the whole world but lose his or her own soul – and in so doing lose the world as well?

NOTES

1. *The Works of Rev. John Wesley* (London: Wesleyan Methodist Book-Room, 1881), vol. i, p. 86.
2. Alister Hardy, *The Spiritual Nature of Man* (Oxford: Clarendon, 1984), p. 1.
3. *The Works of Rev. John Wesley*, op. cit., vol. xi, pp. 340–1.
4. See Frank Whaling, *Christian Theology and World Religions: A Global Approach* (London: Marshall Pickering, 1986), pp. 37–48.
5. See Frank Whaling (ed.), *John and Charles Wesley in the Classics of Western Spirituality* (New York, Ramsey, Toronto: Paulist and London: SPCK), 1981, pp. 8–24.
6. *The Works of Rev. John Wesley*, op. cit., vol. x, p. 68.
7. See Whaling (ed.), *John and Charles Wesley*, op. cit., pp. 24–64.
8. *The Classics of Western Spirituality*, editor: Richard J. Payne, editorial consultant: Ewert H. Cousins (New York, Ramsey, Toronto: Paulist, and London: SPCK, 1978ff); *World Spirituality: An Encyclopedic History of the Religious Quest*, general editor: Ewert H. Cousins (New York: Crossroad, 1985ff).
9. See Frank Whaling (ed.), *Contemporary Approaches to the Study of Religion*, vol. i *The Humanities*, 'The Global Context of the Study of Religion', pp. 436–43 (Berlin, New York, Amsterdam: Mouton, 1983).
10. See Frank Whaling (ed.), *Religion in Today's World*, 'The Emergence of a Global Vision', pp. 21–4 (Edinburgh: T&T Clark, 1987).
11. E. F. Schumacher, *A Guide for the Perplexed* (London: Harper & Row, 1977), p. 127.

12. C. J. Jung, *Collected Works* (Princeton: Princeton University Press, 1969), vol. xi, p. 334, para. 509.

13. C. J. Jung, *Collected Works*, 2nd edn (Princeton: Princeton University Press, 1970), vol. x, p. 202, para. 416. See also C. Bryant, *Jung and the Christian Way* (London: Darton, Longman & Todd, 1983).

14. J. Waardenburg, *Classical Approaches to the Study of Religion* (Berlin, New York, Amsterdam: Mouton, 1981; New York, Berlin: de Gruyter, 1999); F. Whaling (ed.), *Contemporary Approaches to the Study of Religion*, vol. i *The Humanities*, vol. ii *The Social Sciences* (Berlin, New York, Amsterdam: Mouton, 1983), 1984 and *Theory and Method in Religious Studies* (Berlin, New York: de Gruyter, 1995).

15. John Baillie, *A Diary of Private Prayer* (London: Humphrey Milford and Oxford University Press, 1936); Dora Hilda Southgate, *Draw Near to God* (London: Oxford University Press, 1948); Michel Quoist, *Prayers of Life* (Dublin and Melbourne: Gill, 1963); Leslie Weatherhead, *A Private House of Prayer* (London: Hodder & Stoughton, 1958); W. E. Orchard, *The Temple: A Book of Prayers* (London and Toronto: J. M. Dent, 1913); *The Classics of Western Spirituality*, op. cit.

16. See J. L. Mehta in Frank Whaling (ed.), *The World's Religious Traditions: Current Perspectives in Religious Studies* (Edinburgh: T&T Clark, 1984), pp. 33–54.

17. The classical statement is in John Dunne, *The Way of all the Earth* (Notre Dame, Indiana: University of Notre Dame Press, 1978), p. ix.

18. Job 3 verse 26.

19. Teilhard de Chardin, *The Divine Milieu* (New York: Harper & Row, 1968), p. 112.

20. Another way to proceed is to read the book more quickly to begin with and then to use it more slowly and more deeply later on.

21. Prayer is part of the whole person including the body. One can relax each part of the body in turn, starting with the feet and ending with the head. This can even be combined with the approach prayer so that the body and mind can become still together.

22. Control of breathing has been practised by spiritual masters and ordinary people down the ages. It is another way of getting the body and mind in tune so that one's whole being is in the mode of prayer. Regular breathing within a relaxed body enables the body to 'pray' as part of the whole act of praying. Again this can be combined with the approach prayer.

23. This striking phrase appears in Wesley's Minutes of Conference for 1745. See Frank Whaling (ed.), *John and Charles Wesley*, op. cit., p. 57.

Week 1

Monday

APPROACH

Jesus Christ is the same yesterday and today and for ever.

~ Hebrews 13:8 ~

PRAISE

I praise you, Lord, for what you are in your own being. You are beyond the power of my mind fully to comprehend, beyond the resources of my vision fully to realise, beyond the energies of my heart fully to love. I praise you because you are ineffable, O God. Yet you have screwed your greatness down into symbols that I can understand – nails and wood and straw – and for that I praise you.

I praise you, Lord, for what you have been and can be to me: a friend on the way, a master to direct, a sacred light to stir, a solace to comfort, a helper in need, a warner in sloth, a child requiring help, a lover to embrace, a majesty to overpower, a beacon to lead on.

I praise you, Lord, for what I do not yet know of your being and of your relationship to me. I praise you too for what I will never know. Help me to know myself more so that I may praise you more. Grant that in praising you more I may know myself more. Yet praised be you, O God, that however well I may know myself, you surpass my ability to grasp you. Accept the praise of what I have and am now to as much of your being that I glimpse and know now, and to your ineffable love be honour and glory!

THANKS

Though our mouths were full of song as the sea, and our tongues of exultation as the multitude of its waves, and our lips of praise as the wide-extended firmament; though our eyes shone with light like the sun and the moon, and our hands were spread forth like the eagles of heaven, and our feet were as swift as hinds, we should still be unable to thank thee and bless thy name, O Lord our God and God of our fathers, for one thousandth or one ten-thousandth part of the bounties which thou hast bestowed upon our fathers and upon us.

~ Hebrew Morning Service[1] ~

I thank you, Lord, for my fellow men and women. I thank you for those who have little to eat for themselves yet help others. I thank you for those who find it difficult to hope yet press on anyway believing that goodness, beauty and truth bring their own reward. I thank you for those who have been scarred by the power of evil in their own lives yet have not despaired of goodness. I thank you for those who have worked for justice, human rights and non-violence, seemingly in vain, who yet work on.

I thank you for the blessings you have bestowed on me, and ask you to bless my stewardship of them.

SELF-EXAMINATION AND FORGIVENESS

O little self, within whose smallness lies
All that man was, and is, and will become,
Atom unseen that comprehends the skies
And tells the tracks by which the planets roam;
That, without moving, knows the joy of wings,
The tiger's strength, the eagle's secrecy,
And in the hovel can consort with kings,
Or clothe a God with his own mystery.
O with what darkness do we cloak thy light,
What dusty folly gather thee for food,
Thou who alone art knowledge and delight,
The heavenly bread, the beautiful, the good,
O living self, O God, O morning star,
Give us Thy light, forgive us what we are.

~ John Masefield[2] ~

And with this our good Lord said full blissfully, 'Lo, how I loved thee', as if He had said, 'My darling, behold and see thy Lord, thy God that is thy Maker, see what satisfying and bliss I have in thy salvation, and rejoice with Me . . . I died for thee and suffered willingly that which I may. And now is all My bitter pain and all My hard travail turned to endless joy and bliss to Me and to thee.

~ Julian of Norwich[3] ~

MEDITATION

But when you pray, go into your room, close the door and pray to your Father, who is unseen. Then your Father, who sees what is done in secret, will reward you. And when you pray, do not keep on babbling like pagans, for they think they will be heard because of their many words. Do not be like them, for your Father knows what you need before you ask him.

~ Matthew 6:6–8 ~

Before looking at the process of prayer, let us look at the sting in the tail of this meditation. If God knows my needs anyway, why bother putting

Week 1

them to him? We will look at three responses to this question, two of them immediately, and the third in the form of our meditation.

First, as Aquinas put it, 'we must pray, not in order to inform God of our needs and desires, but in order to remind ourselves that in these matters we need divine assistance'. This is alright, but left at this level prayer would remain a form of spiritual self-help, something to do with us rather than God. God knows our needs, but by setting up a personal relationship with God in prayer we enable him to supply our needs in a way that would have been less easy if that personal relationship had not been there.

Both these responses are true. Prayer is beneficial to us, we would be less than human to deny this. It is also a personal relationship with God whereby things can happen to us and to others more easily. However presupposed in these responses is a third reason, found in our meditation, to which we now turn.

Jesus says 'go into your room'. It is one of his few commands. We will see in a moment that 'room' can mean more than a set of four walls, but for most of us a specific room, and often a specific time, is central to prayer. Insofar as Jesus and his friends often did not have private rooms, his habit was to go aside into the hills or elsewhere to be alone with God. We go into our room and shut out our busy world and its daily concerns. We make contact with God. Needs and desires come later. If we have him we have everything.

We go not just into a specific room physically. We go also to an inner room within our mind, and we close the door to the rest of ourselves. We retreat into an inner room deep within ourselves to be alone with God. We do or will find that we can do this elsewhere. When we are busy with other matters, we can, when need or desire arises, tune into the inner room of our being to be with God. To put it another way, we can switch from the everyday world to the spiritual world when necessary. Often it will not be necessary, for the outside world and the people in it are often God's messengers anyway.

We go not just into an interior spiritual room. It is a special room. As St Teresa put it, it is our interior castle. It is a series of interior rooms. It is a place of peace, joy, love and bliss. We don't need to go there – God's presence is available to us anyway – but we want to go there first of all to *be* with our Father, then to express our needs.

PETITION

Father, give to Thy child that which he himself knows not how to ask. I dare not ask either for crosses or consolation; I simply present myself before thee, I open my heart to Thee. Behold my needs which I know not myself; see and do according to Thy tender mercy. Smite or heal, depress or raise me up.

Week 1

I adore all Thy purposes without knowing them.

I am silent; I offer myself in sacrifice.

I yield myself to Thee. I would have no other desire than to accomplish Thy will.

Teach me to pray. Pray Thyself in me.

~ Fénelon[4] ~

PRAYER FOR ACTION

1. *I need not ascend up on high*
   To implore you to come down, O Lord.
   Deep always in my heart you lie
   Challenge and succour to afford.
   But, O! your presence here reveal,
   That I your love and grief may feel!

2. *Within the famine, pain and*
   Death of daily life is your abode.
   You bid the exhausted wounded stand,
   You cry to all 'I share your load –
   Hold high your heads – Your valour show –
   Your Saviour strives for you below!'

3. *Bestir your Spirit in my frame,*
   From dormant sleep my conscience shake!
   My mind exert, my heart inflame,
   My soul enlarge, my zeal awake,
   You to exalt within, without,
   Your cross to show, your joy to shout!

Were I to write an Epilogue like this in the year 2000, I could well look back on the present time as a point when signs of hope were springing forth in all kinds of unexpected places. We have the chance, quite simply, to be the first to live in final accord with our Spaceship Earth – and hence in final harmony with each other. The Ancient Greeks, the Renaissance communities, the founders of America, the Victorians, enjoyed no such challenge as this. What a time to be alive!

~ Epilogue to the *The Gaia Atlas of Planet Management*[5] ~

CONTEMPLATION

Trust in the Lord for ever, for the Lord is the Rock eternal.

~ Isaiah 26:4 ~

Week 1

Tuesday

APPROACH

Forgive us our debts, as we also have forgiven our debtors.

~ Matthew 6:12 ~

PRAISE

This, this is the God I adore,
*   My faithful, unchangeable friend,*
Whose love is as great as his power,
*   And neither knows measure nor end.*

'Tis Jesus, the first and the last,
*   Whose Spirit shall guide me safe home;*
I'll praise him for all that is past,
*   And trust him for all that's to come.*

~ Hymn by Joseph Hart (adapted)[6] ~

I praise God the Father, whose love created me, whose care sustains me, who watches over me eternally, whose light and life are constantly available.

I praise Jesus for his grace, who emptied himself for me, who was tempted in all ways as I am yet without sin, who knew the pain of death, who lives for evermore, who even now prays for me and cares for me.

I praise the Holy Spirit, through whom I have access to the Christian family, whose fellowship renews me, whose witness strengthens me, whose power kindles me, whose insight illumines me, whose silence recollects me.

To you, O God, Father, Son and Holy Spirit be glory and honour forever.

THANKS

I thank you, O Lord, for the gift of forgiveness. I thank you that in your love you have offered an escape from hatred, envy, guilt and anxiety. I thank you that in your love you have opened up access into my inner world. I thank you that in your cross you have given freedom from the past and freedom for the future. I thank you for the pain and self-giving involved in the cross, and that even now you bear the scars of that symbol of forgiveness.

I thank you too, O Lord, for the power to forgive; for the grace to see beyond my own hurt and wounds into the misunderstanding in the heart of another. I thank you for the joy of knowing that patterns of resentment can be broken, that useless doors can be closed and creative doors opened; that healing can ensue.

I thank you for the forgiving power of those who forgive me the wrongs that I have done them; for the forgiving power of fellowship within your community. I thank you for the grace to forgive others, and to accept the forgiveness of others. Yet these again find their possibility and their meaning in the cross from which I hear those words, 'Father forgive them for they know not what they do.'

For the healing power of the cross and for your risen presence, I thank you, O Lord.

> *Hence our hearts melt, our eyes o'erflow.*
> *Our words are lost; nor will we know,*
> > *Nor will we think of aught beside,*
> > *My Lord, my Love is crucified!*
>
> ~ Johann Nitschmann (trans. John Wesley) ~

> *First-born of many brethren thou;*
> *To thee, lo! All our souls we bow;*
> > *To thee our hearts and hands we give;*
> > *Thine may we die, thine may we live!*
>
> ~ Anna Nitschmann (trans. John Wesley)[7] ~

SELF-EXAMINATION AND FORGIVENESS

> *O whoever you are,*
> *who at the word of an insistent servant,*
> *that is your flesh,*
> *by will or act*
> *have shamelessly denied Christ,*
> *who suffered for you,*
> *remember the passion of your beloved Master*
> *and go out with Peter*
> *to weep most bitterly over yourself.*

Week 1

When the one
who looked upon the weeping Peter
looks upon you,
you will be inebriated with the wormwood
of a twofold bitterness:
remorse for yourself
and compassion for Christ,
so that having atoned with Peter
for the guilt of your crime,
with Peter
you will be filled
with the spirit of holiness.

~ St Bonaventure[8] ~

When blessed Mary wip'd her Saviour's feet,
(Whose precepts she had trampled on before)
And wore them for a jewel on her head,
*   Showing his steps should be the street,*
*   Wherein she thenceforth evermore*
With pensive humbleness would live and tread:

She being stain'd herself, why did she strive
To make him clean, who could not be defil'd?
Why kept she not her tears for her own faults,
*   And not his feet? Though we could dive*
*   In tears like seas, our sins are pil'd*
Deeper than they, in words, and works, and thoughts.

Dear soul, she knew who did vouchsafe and deign
To bear her filth; and that her sins did dash
Ev'n God himself: wherefore she was not loath,
*   As she had brought wherewith to stain,*
*   So to bring in wherewith to wash:*
And yet in washing one, she washed both.

~ George Herbert[9] ~

In the year that King Uzziah died, I saw the Lord seated on a throne, high and exalted, and the train of his robe filled the temple. Above him were the seraphs, each with six wings: With two wings they covered their faces, with two they covered their feet, and with two they were flying. And they were calling to one another: 'Holy, holy, holy is the Lord Almighty; the whole earth is full of his glory.' At the sound of their voices the doorposts and thresholds shook and the temple was filled with smoke.

Week 1

37

'Woe to me!' I cried. 'I am ruined! For I am a man of unclean lips, and I live among a people with unclean lips, and my eyes have seen the King, the Lord Almighty.'

Then one of the seraphs flew to me with a live coal in his hand, which he had taken with the tongs from the altar. With it he touched my mouth and said, 'See, this has touched your lips; your guilt is taken away and your sin atoned for'.

Then I heard the voice of the Lord saying, 'Whom shall I send? And who will go for us?'

And I said, 'Here am I. Send me!'

~ Isaiah 6:1–8 ~

MEDITATION

Heaven and earth last forever.
The reason why heaven and earth last forever
is that they do not live for themselves.
Hence, they last forever.

Therefore, the True Person
leaves self behind
and thus is found in front,
is not guarded and thus is preserved,
is self-free and thus is able
to find fulfilment.

~ Tao te ching, vii [10] ~

Then Peter came to Jesus and asked, 'Lord, how many times shall I forgive my brother when he sins against me? Up to seven times?'

Jesus answered, 'I tell you, not seven times, but seventy-seven times.

'Therefore, the kingdom of heaven is like a king who wanted to settle accounts with his servants. As he began the settlement, a man who owed him ten thousand talents was brought to him. Since he was not able to pay, the master ordered that he and his wife and his children and all that he had be sold to repay the debt.

'The servant fell on his knees before him "Be patient with me," he begged, "and I will pay back everything." The servant's master took pity on him, cancelled the debt and let him go.

'But when that servant went out, he found one of his fellow-servants who owed him a hundred denarii. He grabbed him and began to choke him. "Pay back what you owe me!" he demanded.

'His fellow-servant fell to his knees and begged him, "Be patient with me, and I will pay you back."

'But he refused. Instead, he went off and had the man thrown into prison until he could pay the debt. When the other servants saw what had happened, they were greatly distressed and went and told their master everything that had happened.

Week 1

'Then the master called the servant in. "You wicked servant," he said, "I cancelled all that debt of yours because you begged me to. Shouldn't you have had mercy on your fellow-servant just as I had on you?"'

~ St Matthew 18:21–33 ~

'Forgiveness is the beggar's refuge; we must pay back our debts,' so the saying goes. The glory of the Gospel is that this saying is not true. We can obtain free forgiveness for our sin.

This is not the same as saying that forgiveness is easy or cheap. Just how costly forgiveness is we find when we gaze at Christ on the cross. Just how much it costs God to grant us free forgiveness for our sins we see when we hear the words of Jesus saying, 'Father, forgive them, for they know not what they do!' There, with Christ crucified, we see what our sin really means to a righteous God, and there at the same time we receive free forgiveness for our sin.

However, in the Lord's Prayer there is a qualification. It says, 'Forgive us our debts, as we also have forgiven our debtors.' The test of our receiving the forgiveness of God is our own willingness to forgive others the wrongs they have done us. Jesus said this, and he stressed it time and time again.

In this story, a king has two servants. The first one owes him a fortune. There is no chance of him repaying this debt. So he asks the king to wipe it out. And in the end the king agrees to cancel the whole of that tremendous debt. The servant goes out free.

He meets another servant who owes him a small debt, and the first servant demands payment of this small sum that is owed to him. The second servant begs for time to pay. The first servant is adamant – he requires payment now! So harsh is he that he has the other servant thrown into prison.

When the king hears about this incident he is livid. He calls the first servant in front of him and says to him, 'You fool! I forgave you the whole of that enormous debt! You could not possibly have paid it no matter how much time you had! Yet here is someone else who owes you a small amount, and will you let him off and forgive him? No, you will not! You fool!'

And let us be honest. Often God says to us, You fool! I forgave you your sin, a debt you could not have repaid yourself. Yet here is someone against whom you have a grudge, or an imagined grudge, and will you forgive them? No, you will not! You fool!

Yet it is not easy to forgive others. It is not easy to forgive what may be the patterns of half a lifetime. It is not easy to forgive that which is fudged or half-buried in the twilight of our being. It is not easy to forgive those who misrepresent us, or slander us, or actively harm us. We end up where we began – with the cross of Christ. There, we receive both the forgiveness of God and the power to forgive others.

Forgiveness is not the beggar's refuge. It is the hallmark of a courageous person. For we know that when we tread the road of God's forgiveness, we

Week 1

also embark upon the adventure of forgiving others. They work together. They are two halves of the same coin. They are complementary. Forgiveness and forgivingness are the in and out, the yin and yang, of the committed life. Life can never be the same again. Having put our hand to the plough of forgiveness, there is no turning back!

PETITION

I pray, O Lord, for the gift of forgiveness in my own life. So often I receive it glibly as though it were of passing worth. Sometimes in my proud moods I refuse to accept it because I feel there is an abyss separating me from yourself due to the immensity of my sin. I know that you do forgive me, O Lord. The fault lies in my inability to receive, not in your unwillingness to give. Open the floodgates of my heart to the depths of your forgiveness. May I know your forgiveness deep in my life and deep in my being. May I, with Mary Magdalene of old, love much because I have been forgiven much!

Help me to forgive others, O Lord. Slough off the inferiority, envy, pride and stubbornness that prevent me from forgiving. Grant me such a vision of what Christ has done for me that resentment against others for the wrongs they have done me can be transformed through the cleansing power of a greater affection. Help me, O Lord, to forgive others without condoning the offences they have done just as you have forgiven me without condoning my offences. In your life may I receive and give life, in your love may I receive and give love, in your cross may I receive and give forgiveness. While we were yet sinners, you died for us. Help me to live a forgiving life because I know myself forgiven. Forgive me my debts, as also I have forgiven my debtors.

PRAYER FOR ACTION

A Creed for Calcutta

Glory to you God. I believe in you.
I believe that you are Holy and One and Just.
I believe that you are the Creator of all things and that you have given
    man dominion over all your created world.
I believe in one world full of riches meant for everyone to enjoy.
I believe in one race, the Family of Man. I affirm that each man is my
    brother and we are responsible for each other.
I believe that we must seek to build a society where there is social,
    economic and religious freedom.
I believe in Jesus and the Bible's evidence about him, whose life, death and
    resurrection prove God's permanent love for the world.

Week 1

I believe in the purpose of God to unite in Christ everything spiritual and secular, and because I believe in this I commit myself to working with all men of good will to bring about God's revelation of love in this place.

CONTEMPLATION

While we were sinners, Christ died for us.

~ Romans 5:8 ~

Week 1

Wednesday

APPROACH

I have come that you may have life, and have it to the full.

~ John 10:10 ~

PRAISE

1. *How shall I sing that majesty*
   Which angels do admire?
   Let dust in dust and silence lie;
   Sing, sing, ye heavenly choir.
   Thousands of thousands stand around
   Thy throne, O God most high;
   Ten thousand times ten thousand sound
   Thy praise, but who am I?

2. *Thy brightness unto them appears,*
   Whilst I thy footsteps trace;
   A sound of God comes to my ears,
   But they behold thy face.
   They sing because thou art their Sun;
   Lord, send a beam on me;
   For where heav'n is but once begun
   There alleluias be.

3. *How great a being, Lord, is thine,*
   Which doth all beings keep!
   Thy knowledge is the only line
   To sound so vast a deep.
   Thou art a sea without a shore,
   A sun without a sphere;
   Thy time is now and evermore,
   Thy place is everywhere.

~ John Mason[11] ~

Week 1

THANKS

We thank you, Lord, for all the ways in which you have shown yourself to us.

We thank you for your presence in nature: for the song of a bird, the lilt of a mountain, the colour of a flower, the joy of animals with their young.

We thank you for your coming through other humans: for the laughter of children, the care of mothers, the love of families, the concern of neighbours, the thoughtfulness of friends.

We thank you for your coming to us in the small things of life: for washing up, for lessons, for leisure, for imagination, for play.

We thank you for the eternal values that mediate your presence: for the beauty of Everest and the music of Mozart, for truth in science, literature and art, for goodness in St Francis, in the Buddha and in your sages of every age, religion and culture.

We thank you for your coming to us through the prophets of old, through the saints of today, through Jesus who was called Immanuel, God with us.

We thank you for the kingdom of God within us.

Save us, Lord, from so reaching for the stars and planets afar that we turn away from the universe that is within our own life where you are waiting to communicate with us if we will let you.

We thank you, Lord, for your grace in coming to us in so many different ways. When we forget you, you do not forget us; when we scorn you, you do not scorn us. For your coming to us always with a love that will not let us go, we thank you, O Lord!

SELF-EXAMINATION AND FORGIVENESS

Now I am at rest with you, O Self!
There was a time when we were strangers
To each other, eyeing from afar,
Like passing yachts, the mutual call
To intimacy. Sense was there none
In coming close, nor reason to cry
Out 'Be still that I may know you!'
Apart were we indeed, though linked in germ,
Unwed nor even yet betrothed.

The passing round went on apace
Within the outer world, engaging
Long, and with full force, the flowing
Surge of action, skill and bounding
Life. I wist not why a hidden
Ache warned 'think' – and then I knew!

Week 1

My self was lost, or rather not yet
Found! Of soul the labyrinthine depths
Were hid as though existing not!

And so your whisper came into my heart,
O Self, at first how still and soft
In tone, as though afraid to intrude
Into the portals opening gently
To your sway! And then more urgent
Was your call, disturbing fast the
Tenor of my ways – till now my
Peace with you is found! No more can I
My Self ignore, Life of my life!

Now I am at rest with you, O Self!

MEDITATION

Now there is in Jerusalem near the Sheep Gate a pool, which in Aramaic is
called Bethesda. Here a great number of disabled people used to lie – the
blind, the lame, the paralysed. One who was there had been an invalid for
thirty-eight years. When Jesus saw him lying there and learned that he had
been in that condition for a long time, he asked him, 'Do you want to get well?'

'Sir,' the invalid replied, 'I have no-one to help me into the pool when the
water is stirred. While I am trying to get in, someone else goes down ahead of
me.'

Then Jesus said to him, 'Get up! Pick up your mat and walk'. At once the man
was cured; he picked up his mat and walked.

~ John 5:2–9 ~

In imagination I go back to Jerusalem. I wander through the streets
bewildered by the variety of sounds and smells. On a piece of level ground
there is a pool of water and some porches. They offer relief from the heat
of the day. I walk over.

The pool is in the centre surrounded by five covered porches. Attendants
are trying to keep them clean but it is difficult because there are so many
people there. In spite of the crowd it is an attractive place.

I notice that many of the people seem to be unwell. They are of different
ages. Some are surrounded by helpers, others are alone. Many of them
seem to be assembled near the pool. Suddenly there is a ripple of water near
the edge of the pool. There is rapid action as the invalids are helped down
into the water to absorb its rippling health.

I see that one man is alone. He seems forlorn and I go to him. 'I have
been like this for thirty-eight years,' he explains. 'My nephew brings me

Week 1

in the morning but he has to work and I cannot make it to the pool when the water moves.' My heart goes out to him and I resolve to help.

I am just about to offer my services when I see someone else coming over. I had noticed him already while I was speaking to the man. He holds the attention, and efforts are made to slow him down and speak to him. But he has seen that my man is alone and he is on his way over. I step aside but I listen.

He says that his name is Jesus, and he engages my man in conversation. In a very short time he finds out about the man. The man warms to his kindly smile and piercing eyes and opens up his heart in a way that had not happened with me. He is absorbed in Jesus and taken out of himself. I seem to understand him better, too.

Suddenly Jesus says to him, 'Do you want to get well?' He hesitates and says that he cannot reach the water at the right time to get well but he seems to be unconvinced by his own words and thrown into a new state of mind. Jesus tells him to pick up his mat and walk. The man smiles, and frowns, and smiles, and tries – and it works!

The man has gone, and Jesus and I are alone. We talk about the man and Jesus asks about myself. I, too, am thrown into a new state of mind. I realise that I am not physically ill but neither am I whole. Jesus says to me, 'Do you want to be whole?' I make some excuse but am unconvinced by my own words. It is a moment of decision. Do I want to be made whole with the consequences attendant on that? Before I can even say, 'Yes,' Jesus says 'Pick up your mat and walk.'

PETITION

1. *O God, for ever old yet new,*
   In every age your calling true
   In novel ways unfolds;
   Help us at this centennial time
   To tap the millenarian mine
   Your providence upholds!

2. *A vision of a global world*
   Environmentally renewed
   Within our soul sustain!
   Humanely linked by love and care,
   May all your children everywhere
   New empathy attain!

3. *As beauty, wisdom, truth and love*
   With sloth and fear and malice strive
   Your victory to trace;

Week 1

Unlock the gate, yourself the key,
That opens unto liberty
For all the human race!

4. *May I, within the total frame*
   Evolving in the world's domain,
   Old energies renew!
   My life – not mine but yours, O Lord –
   Bestowed on me, to you restored,
   Be energised by you![12]

PRAYER FOR ACTION

Go placidly amid the noise and haste, and remember what peace there may be in silence. As far as possible without surrender be on good terms with all persons. Speak your truth quietly and clearly; and listen to others, even the dull and the ignorant; for they have their day. Avoid loud and aggressive persons, they are vexations to the spirit. If you compare yourself to others, you may become vain and bitter; for always there will be greater and lesser persons than yourself. Enjoy your achievements as well as your plans. Keep interested in your career, however humble; it is a real possession in the changing fortunes of time. Exercise caution on your business affairs; for the world is full of trickery. But let this not blind you to what virtue there is; many persons strive for high ideals; and everywhere life is full of heroism. Be yourself. Especially, do not feign affection. Neither be cynical about love; for in the face of all aridity and disenchantment it is perennial like the grass. Take kindly the counsel of the years, gratefully surrendering the things of youth. Nurture strength of spirit to shield you in sudden misfortune. But do not stress yourself with imaginings. Many fears are born of fatigue and loneliness. Beyond a wholesome discipline be gentle with yourself. You are a child of the universe, no less than the trees and the stars; you have a right to be here. And whether or not it is clear to you, no doubt the universe is unfolding as it should. Therefore be at peace with God, whatever you conceive Him to be, and whatever your labours and aspirations in the noisy confusion of life keep peace with your soul. With all its strain, drudgery and broken dreams, it is still a beautiful world. Be careful. Strive to be happy.

~ Baltimore, 1692[13] ~

Friendship is fashioned when in trust
   Those who before have ne'er been thrust
(By chance forespent) into the light
   Of mutual knowledge, sealed in sight,
Become aware that neath the veil
   Of outward vesture, racial tale,
a texture lurks, form deep transcending,
   Whose awesome promise is unending.

Week 1

What is it then: this word, this hope,
This harbinger of kindness gilt
With passion cast upon the veldt?
Blind atoms' play? Nay surely more
The leap of hearts that celebrate
With joy a oneness truly felt.

He prayeth well, who loveth well
Both man and bird and beast.
He prayeth best, who loveth best
All things both great and small;
For the dear God who loveth us,
He made and loveth all.

~ Samuel Taylor Coleridge[14] ~

CONTEMPLATION

Simplicity is the pearl of the Gospel.

Week 1

Thursday

My chief end is to glorify God and enjoy him for ever.

PRAISE

I praise you, O Lord, for all the glimpses I have had of your redeeming love. I praise you for your beauty shown forth in the world: for mountains and valleys, for gardens and rivers, for fish and birds, for our mother earth. I praise you for the handiwork of human hands: for cars, and electric lights, for houses and clothes, for things that enrich my daily living. I praise you for the gift of people: for those who serve my needs and refresh my soul, for family and friends, for those saints who have mirrored your love. I praise you that you have not left yourself without a witness in the whole earth: that in all the world's religions there is evidence of your glory. I praise you for the times of your appearing in the interior castle of my heart: for the beatific sight albeit seen through a glass dimly. I praise you for yourself, your love, and your glory.

1. *Meet and right it is to sing,*
    In every time and place,
  Glory to our heavenly King,
      The God of truth and grace.
  Join we then with sweet accord,
      All in one thanksgiving join:
  Holy, holy, holy, Lord,
      Eternal praise be thine!

2. *Thee the firstborn sons of light,*
    In choral symphonies,
  Praise by day, day without night,
      And never, never cease;
  Angels and archangels all
      Praise the mystic Three in One,
  Sing, and stop, and gaze, and fall
      O'erwhelmed before thy throne.

Week 1

3. *Vying with that happy choir*
      Who chant thy praise above,
   We on eagles' wings aspire,
      The wings of faith and love;
   Thee they sing with glory crowned,
      We extol the slaughtered Lamb;
   Lower if our voices sound
      Our subject is the same.

4. *Father, God, thy love we praise*
      Which gave thy Son to die;
   Jesus, full of truth and grace,
      Alike we glorify;
   Spirit, Comforter divine,
      Praise by all to thee be given,
   Till we in full chorus join,
      And earth is turned to heaven.

$\sim$ Charles Wesley[15] $\sim$

THANKS

And so I was taught that love is our Lord's meaning. And I saw very certainly in this and in everything that before God made us he loved us, which love was never abated and never will be. And in this love he has done all his works, and in this love he had made all things profitable to us, and in this love our life is everlasting. In our creation we had beginning, but the love in which he created us was in him without beginning. In this love we have our beginning, and all this shall we see in God without end. Thanks be to God.

$\sim$ Julian of Norwich[16] $\sim$

1. *The Lord is my shepherd, I shall not be in want.*
2. *He makes me lie down in green pastures,*
   he leads me beside quiet waters,
3.   *he restores my soul.*
   He guides me in paths of righteousness
      for his name's sake.
4. *Even though I walk*
      through the valley of the shadow of death,
   I will fear no evil,
      for you are with me;
   your rod and your staff,
      they comfort me.

Week 1

5. *You prepare a table before me*
    in the presence of my enemies.
 You anoint my head with oil;
    my cup overflows.
6. *Surely goodness and love will follow me*
    all the days of my life,
 And I will dwell in the house of the Lord
    for ever.

~ Psalm 23 ~

SELF-EXAMINATION AND FORGIVENESS

Every Christian, every religious person, is called to be a saint. But what is a saint? Is a saint someone who sets out to reform himself? Surely only in part, if at all. Is a saint someone who sets out on a crusade to arrange the world and solve its problems? Surely only in part, if at all. Is a saint someone who sets out to save himself? Surely only in part, if at all. Is a saint someone who sets out to cultivate his garden of prayer by rooting out the weeds and producing flowers? Surely only in part, if at all. Reform, crusades to transform the world, salvation, prayerfulness are the fruits of saintliness rather than its grounds. Sanctity is an end that is grounded in God, and only to that extent is it an end in itself.

Jesus has many who love his kingdom in heaven, but few who bear his cross. He has many who desire comfort, but few who desire suffering. He finds many to share his feast, but few his fasting. All desire to rejoice with him, but few are willing to suffer for his sake. Many follow Jesus to the breaking of bread, but few to the drinking of the cup of passion. Many admire his miracles, but few follow him to the humiliation of his cross. Many love Jesus as long as no hardship touches them ...

They who love Jesus for his own sake, and not for the sake of comfort for themselves, bless him in every trial and anguish of heart, no less than in the greatest joy. And were he never willing to bestow comfort on them, they would still always praise him and give him thanks.

~ Thomas à Kempis[17] ~

I am no longer my own, but yours. Put me to what you will, rank me with whom you will; put me to doing, put me to suffering; let me be employed for you or laid aside for you, exalted for you or brought low for you; let me be full, let me be empty; let me have all things, let me have nothing; I freely and heartily yield all things to your pleasure and disposal.

And now, O glorious and blessed God, Father, Son and Holy Spirit, you are mine, and I am yours. So be it. And the Covenant which I have made on earth, let it be ratified in heaven.

~ Methodist Covenant Service[18] ~

Week 1

MEDITATION

Then the chief cupbearer said to Pharaoh, 'Today I am reminded of my shortcomings. Pharaoh was once angry with his servants, and he imprisoned me and the chief baker I the house of the captain of the guard. Each of us had a dream the same night, and each dream has a meaning of its own. Now a young Hebrew was there with us, a servant of the captain of the guard. We told him our dreams, and he interpreted them for us, giving each man the interpretation of his dream. And things turned out exactly as he interpreted them to us: I was restored to my position, and the other man was hanged.'

So Pharaoh sent for Joseph, and he was quickly brought from the dungeon. When he had shaved and changed his clothes, he came before Pharaoh.

Pharaoh said to Joseph, 'I had a dream, and no-one can interpret it. But I have heard it said of you that when you hear a dream you can interpret it.'

'I cannot do it,' Joseph replied to Pharaoh, 'but God will give Pharaoh the answer he desires.'

~ Genesis 41:9–16 ~

Joseph is at rock bottom. He is languishing in prison. His fate is in the hands of others, and it is only a pang of conscience on the part of the chief cupbearer that brings a glimmer of hope to his situation. Had he done the decent thing the cupbearer would have helped Joseph on his release. Now, better late than never, he remembers the young Hebrew, still locked in prison, who had interpreted his own dream.

Joseph had always been a 'dreamer'. He had always been able to go inward as well as live outwardly; he had always had contact with the feminine side of his being as well as engaging in the activities appropriate to his manhood. Indeed his ability to interpret dreams, which would stand him in good stead now, had been a prime cause of his early downfall. It had given him psychic access to God. The problem was that he had used it with arrogance. He was the big 'I Am'. His forecasts that his brothers' sheafs would surround his, and that they would bow down to him, although true, were not destined to make him popular with his brothers, nor was the fact that he was the favourite son of his father Jacob.

Thus there had developed the course of events that had led his brothers to conspire against him. Instead of being killed, he had been put in a pit and thence transported into Egypt. Slavery had been succeeded by service in Potiphar's household. Ironically, Joseph's faithfulness in resisting the advances of Potiphar's wife had led to his present predicament of prison, and the invitation to interpret Pharaoh's dream.

It is now a different Joseph. He still has the ability to interpret dreams, he still has inwardness, he still has a balance within his personality, but he does not say 'You bet I can interpret this or any other dream you care to throw at me.' He says, 'I cannot do it but God will give Pharaoh the answer

Week 1

he desires.' He has the ability to interpret dreams, yet he does not have it, God has it within him. Joseph retains his gifts but they have been tempered by suffering and given into the hands of God.

All of us are unique. We have unique gifts. Some of us are 'dreamers', others are not; some of us are practically oriented, others are not; some live more by analysis, others more by intuition; some have a direct sense of the world without, others have an immediate awareness of the world within. God uses the gifts that *we* have. He does not want us to be anyone else. But he does want us to develop *our* gifts. He wants us to love ourselves not through self-love but for his sake. When we see ourselves and our gifts in an arrogant way like Joseph did (and his gifts were many), our effectiveness is affected. When we see ourselves as having gifts we do not have, or courting gifts we do not have, or seeing the gifts of others in the light of our own, our effectiveness is equally affected. Part of loving God is loving the self that we are becoming for his sake.

Things turned out well for Joseph in the end. Luck went his way, or perhaps he made his own luck. And even if no cupbearer had remembered his gift of interpretation of dreams, Joseph would have found another providential way along another escape route, or even by staying in prison. For he was right with himself and right with God and right with his own talents. What more can we ask of ourselves and of others?

PETITION

Teach us, good Lord, to serve thee as thou deservest; to give and not to count the cost; to fight and not to heed the wounds; to toil and not to seek for rest; to labour and not to ask for any reward save knowing that we do thy will.

~ Ignatius of Loyola[19] ~

PRAYER FOR ACTION

To love life and men as God loves them – for the sake of their
    infinite possibilities,
to wait like Him
to judge like Him
without passing judgment,
to obey the order when it is given
and never look back –
then He can use you – then, PERHAPS, He will use you. And if He
    doesn't use you – what matter. In His hand
every moment has its meaning, its greatness, its glory, its peace, its
    co-inherence.

~ Dag Hammarskjold[20] ~

Week 1

CONTEMPLATION

I no longer live, but Christ lives in me.

~ Galatians 2:20 ~

Week 1

Friday

APPROACH

God be merciful to me a sinner.

~ Luke 18:13 ~

PRAISE

I praise and honour and adore you here and everywhere, now and at all times.

I praise you for human courage: for millions who live in conditions of despair with dignity and even with joy; for all out of every nation and religion who seek to enhance others and to enrich the world's store of love; for those who live in pain and endure it triumphantly.

I praise you for Christ's death and resurrection, and for the Holy Spirit shed abroad in the world, for your Gospel that the broken-hearted will be renewed, the prisoners freed, the fearful given hope, and the little ones fed in your name.

I praise you for faith, and hope shed abroad in the world and shed abroad in my heart: a faith, love and hope so simple that they pass understanding. All praise be to you, O God.

THANKS

Lord, thank you for listening to me – to my thoughts, to my grandiose visions, to my illusions, to my rebellions, to my hypocrisies and to my attempts to be honest with myself.

You listen to me when I don't listen to you. You listen to what I don't say as well as to what I do say. You listen to my heart as well as to my mind. You listen to my intent as well as to my achievement. You listen to my heartache as well as to my arrogance. You listen with full attention, with absolute patience, and with overflowing love.

Lord, teach me how to listen: to leaves, and birds, and the wind; to the voices, dreams and hopes of my fellows; and to you, O Lord.

Insofar as I can only listen with as much of myself as I know to as much of yourself as I know, help me to know myself better that in listening more deeply to my own heart I may hear you more and more, until the time comes when I hear, yet it is not I but you who heareth within me.

Week 1

1. *He wants not friends that hath thy love,*
   And may converse and walk with thee,
   And with thy saints here and above,
   With whom for ever I must be.

2. *In the communion of thy saints*
   Is wisdom, safety and delight;
   And when my heart declines and faints,
   'Tis raised by their heat and light.

3. *As for my friends, they are not lost;*
   The several vessels of thy fleet,
   Though parted now, by tempests tossed,
   Shall safely in the haven meet.

4. *Still are we centred all in thee,*
   Members, though distant, of one Head;
   In the same family are we,
   By the same faith and Spirit led.

5. *Before thy throne we daily meet*
   As joint-petitioners to thee;
   In spirit we each other greet,
   And shall again each other see.

6. *The heavenly hosts, world without end,*
   Shall be my company above;
   And thou, my best and surest friend,
   Who shall divide me from thy love?

~ Richard Baxter[21] ~

SELF-EXAMINATION AND FORGIVENESS

I did not think, I did not strive,
The deep peace burnt my me alive;
The bolted door had broken in,
I knew that I had done with sin.
I knew that Christ had given me birth
To brother all the souls on earth,
And every bird and every beast
Should share the crumbs broke at the feast.
O glory of the lighted mind,
How dead I'd been, how dumb, how blind.
The station brook to my new eyes,
Was babbling out of Paradise,
The waters rushing from the rain
Were singing Christ has risen again.

Week 1

I thought all earthly creatures knelt
From rapture of the joy I felt.
The narrow station-wall's brick ledge,
The wild hop withering in the hedge,
The lights in huntsman's upper storey
Were parts of an eternal glory,
Were God's eternal garden flowers.
I stood in bliss at this for hours.

O wet red swathe of earth laid bare,
O truth, O strength, O gleaming share,
O patient eyes that watch the goal,
O ploughman of the sinner's soul.
O Jesus, drive the coulter deep
To plough my living man from sleep.

~ John Masefield[22] ~

MEDITATION

Therefore I tell you, do not worry about your life, what you will eat or drink; or about your body, what you will wear. Is not life more important than food, and the body more important than clothes? Look at the birds of the air; they do not sow or reap or store away in barns and yet your heavenly Father feeds them. Are you not much more valuable than they? Who of you by worrying can add a single hour to his life?

But seek first his kingdom and his righteousness, and all these things will be given to you as well. Therefore do not worry about tomorrow, for tomorrow will worry about itself. Each day has enough trouble of its own.

~ Matthew 6:25–7, 33–4 ~

At first sight this passage doesn't apply to me. It seems more suited to my happy-go-lucky extrovert friends who seem to waltz through life without a care in the world. It seems more suited to the bachelor or spinster, the monk or nun, who are often less bound up with insurance and mortgages and the like. It seems more suited to those detached souls who never seem to think about the threat of nuclear war, or ecological disaster, or those suffering from famine and injustice.

But it is no good. I know that this is an excuse that doesn't work. Extroverts, nuns and detached souls are not necessarily putting God's kingdom first; introverts, married people and those concerned to be involved in the world's affairs may have God's kingdom at the centre of their lives.

What is at the centre of my life? Perhaps, if I am honest, a cluster of things are near the centre: my family, my job, my desire for a deeper spirituality, my concern for global problems. The list seems to be endless.

Week 1

But wait a minute! Perhaps that is the point! These concerns are not necessarily wrong. Perhaps I need a deeper concern for my family, for my job, for a deeper life, for the world's problems. Jesus seems to be pointing me to my basic perspective. What is the first thing, what is the axis around which my life revolves, what is my ultimate preoccupation?

Perhaps I am not really sure – it seems to be moving the whole time. Yet is that a bad thing? Perhaps not, I would have to be a holy person in 24-hour contemplation to be constantly centred on the kingdom of God.

But I know that this is a get-out as well. I need a centre for all my concerns, a framework on to which I can hang the pegs of my family, my work, my spiritual life, my social and political involvement, my hobbies, my imagination. Jesus says 'seek first his kingdom', put it first and other things will be given to you as well. But it really means a switch in priorities, a switch in my world-view.

It won't happen all at once, in a moment of time. But it can start today. It can start now. Let it become my centre and core into which other things fit, rather than the other way round. I put my hand into the hand of God. More and more I will remember that it is there, and more and more I will be sure that he can never let it go.

PETITION

The time of business does not with me differ from the time of prayer; and in the noise and clatter of my kitchen, while several persons are at the same time calling for different things, I possess God in as great tranquillity as if I were upon my knees at the blessed sacrament.

~ Brother Lawrence[23] ~

O Lord, I cannot be like Brother Lawrence. You would not want me to be like him. But grant me a measure of his spirit that in the circumstances of my life I may see your kingdom at work and I may put it first.

PRAYER FOR ACTION

Four Global Commands

Love your God with heart, soul, mind and strength.
Love your neighbour as yourself.
Love one another as I have loved you.
Love your planet earth and care for it.

They came consumed with hunger,
And we cradled them and fed them.

58

He came with anguished sores,
Unable to conceal his cries,
And we nursed his hurt and bound his wounds.

She came assailed by anger,
Afflicted by the turmoil
That enraged her bloodshot eyes,
And we cleared her sight and cleansed her vision.
The little one came beset by care,
Bewildered, frightened, undone
By deeds of evil that his mind
Could not encompass, not as yet,
And we turned his gaze on high.

They seemed to come forever,
And to never, never stop,
As come they did to cry, to moan, to curse.

The voice welled up within me,
Will they always, always come,
Will their tumult never cease,
Will the flow go on forever,
Will the end be never nigh,
Will a rest be always near yet far?

Another voice came to me,
Surrounding me with calm
And filling me with joy,
Directing me to look within.
And as I looked that same voice said,
The needs will never cease,
Suffering will always come,
For you and me the rest will
Always lie ahead, the work will
Never end – but I am with you
Ever till heaven and earth shall cease.

CONTEMPLATION

Whatever you did for one of the least of these brothers of mine,
you did for me.

~ Matthew 25:40 ~

Week 1

Saturday

The eternal God is your refuge
and underneath are the everlasting arms.

~ Deuteronomy 33:27 ~

PRAISE

1. *Praise to the living God!*
   All praised be his name,
   Who was, and is, and is to be,
   For aye the same!
   The one eternal God
   Ere aught that now appears:
   The First, the Last, beyond all thought
   His timeless years!

2. *Formless, all lovely forms*
   Declare his loveliness;
   Holy, no holiness of earth
   Can his express.
   Lo, he is Lord of all!
   Creation speaks his praise,
   And everywhere, above, below,
   His will obeys.

3. *His Spirit floweth free,*
   High surging where it will:
   In prophet's word he spoke of old,
   He speaketh still.
   Established is his law,
   And changeless it shall stand,
   Deep writ upon the human heart,
   On sea, on land.

Week 1

4. *Eternal life hath he*
      Implanted in the soul;
   His love shall be our strength and stay,
      While ages roll.
   Praise to the living God!
      All praised be his name,
   Who was, and is, and is to be,
      For aye the same.

~ medieval Jewish doxology (trans. Landsberg and Mann)[24] ~

THANKS

I thank Thee, Lord, for knowing me better than I know myself, and for letting me know myself better than others know me.

Make me, I pray, better than they suppose, and forgive me for what they do not know.

~ Abu Bakr[25] ~

I knew Him by revelation, as He who hath the key did open, and as the Father of Life drew me to His Son by the Spirit. And then the Lord did gently lead me along, and did let me see His love, which was endless and eternal. He gave me His light to believe in, and gave me hope, revealed himself in me, and gave me His Spirit and His grace, which I found sufficient in the deeps and in weakness. Thus, in the greatest sorrows and temptations that many times beset me, the Lord in His mercy did keep me.

~ From the *Journal* of George Fox[26] ~

I thank you, Lord, for your love, which is bringing sweetness to my heart, strength to my will, generosity to my mind, healing to my body, vision to my eyes, and nourishment to my soul.

I thank you too for the gift of prayer whereby your plenitude of love is brought down into my small heart, and my spiritual desire is taken up into your fullness.

I thank you for your love for me, and my yearning for you, and for their coming together now.

SELF-EXAMINATION AND FORGIVENESS

I come before you in confession, Lord. Help me to open my heart to you, and to receive your forgiveness.

I confess to laziness and tiredness, which come from a lack of constant purpose rather than exhaustion. I confess to speaking about others in ways that may be unhelpful to them. I confess to harbouring thoughts of jealousy and ill-will in regard to others. I confess to greed for unnecessary

Week 1

things and vanity for unnecessary fame. I confess to falsehoods and indulgences the more subtle because they are small and hidden. I confess to drift and staleness in my life. I confess to meanness of spirit and a grudging attitude to forgiveness.

Burn up, I pray, the dross of my life, and recharge me by the power of your forgiveness. May I know your forgiveness now deep in my heart and deep in my life, and, being forgiven, may I see more deeply the need for ongoing forgiveness through the healing power of your love.

MEDITATION

Meanwhile, the older son was in the field. When he came near the house, he heard music and dancing. So he called one of the servants and asked him what was going on. 'Your brother has come,' he replied, 'and your father has killed a fattened calf because he has him back safe and sound.'

The older brother became angry and refused to go in. So his father went out and pleaded with him. But he answered his father, 'Look! All these years I've been slaving for you and never disobeyed your orders. Yet you never gave me even a young goat so I could celebrate with my friends. But when this son of yours who has squandered your property with prostitutes comes home, you kill the fattened calf for him!'

'My son,' the father said, 'you are always with me, and everything I have is yours. But we had to celebrate and be glad, because this brother of yours was dead and is alive again; he was lost and is found!'

~ Luke 15:25–32 ~

In this story attention has often been focused upon the younger brother. It is equally likely that we are the elder brother. We have toed the line and done the things that needed to be done. We have given attention to our parents. We have lived a good life. This is not just our opinion: other people tell us so. We have kept up standards. We have genuinely tried to do the right thing at various times in our life according to our lights. We have been useful and solid and trustworthy.

Now we are hopping mad. This member of the family who went off the rails and loafed around and went with prostitutes – this renegade has found his way home. And what happens? He gets a tremendous party organised for him! We never had a party like this, and we never did anything wrong! Our rage is irrational, but it is there. Why?

One reason we can state and then dismiss. Some irritation is natural with the best will in the world. It is rooted in human nature, ours and everyone else's. A complete lack of irritation would be either very saintly or somewhat disturbing.

A deeper reason for our anger may well be pride. We have lived a good life but it has been too centred on ourselves. Instead of thanking God for our many blessings, we have attributed them to ourselves. Instead of generosity towards others, we have been careful and cautious towards

Week 1

them. We have been afraid to be ourselves. We have directed towards others the frustration we really felt with ourselves.

We may even feel a hidden admiration for our relative that we scarcely dare to admit. They had the courage to try and find themselves even if it didn't work out too well. We kept on the same old path out of habit or laziness or lack of adventure rather than out of conviction. We had the satisfaction of arguing that we were a cut above our relative, but this looming party even raises questions about what we thought was that certainty. What is our father playing at?

We may even feel a battle within ourselves. There is an adventurous rake in us waiting to find expression (although hopefully not in such an extravagant way!) and we have repressed part of ourselves that could have found a wholesome outlet and we are reaping the reward.

Whatever the reason for our anger, and there may be other reasons peculiar to us, our father's remark strikes home into our heart. It points us to God who is reflected in this story. 'You are always with me, and everything I have is yours,' he says.

Can this really be true? Is God always with us? Is everything he has really ours? I offer my anger at my relative – and my father – to God. I offer my past sedate life to God; it may not have been much but he knows I tried. I offer my unexplored gifts to God including the adventurous streak I may have suppressed. I offer my relative to God. I offer myself to God.

I hear a voice saying, 'We must celebrate and be glad, because your relative was lost and is found – and you were lost and are found!'

PETITION

The quality of mercy is not strained;
It droppeth as the gentle rain from heaven
Upon the place beneath. It is twice blest;
It blesseth him that gives and him that takes.
'Tis mightiest in the mightiest; it becomes
The throned monarch better than his crown.
His sceptre shows the force of temporal power,
The attribute to awe and majesty,
Wherein doth sit the dread and fear of kings;
But mercy is above this scept'red sway;
It is enthroned in the heart of kings,
It is an attribute of God himself,
And earthly power doth then show likest God's
When mercy seasons justice.

~ William Shakespeare[27] ~

1. *O name and form beyond all forms,*
        I seek your face to see;
    Object abstruse of learned tomes,
        Have you a smile for me?

2. *Along the ways I've searched your trace,*
        Your track I've pondered long;
    In hill and vale has peeped your face,
        When will I sing your song?

3. *Then, lo! The switch comes on! I know*
        'Twas you who searchest me;
    In mount and book you spoke and said,
        'In me you live and see!'

4. *How patient, gentle, long and true*
        Hung high the crucified;
    Proclaiming, every heartbeat through,
        'I at your door abide!'

5. *Unlocked the bolts are of my heart,*
        My search continues still;
    Propeller of my growing love,
        Your life in mine fulfil!'

PRAYERS FOR ACTION

The most beautiful object I have ever seen in a photograph, in all my life, is the planet Earth seen from the distance of the moon, hanging there in space, obviously alive. Although it seems at first glance to be made up of innumerable separate species of living things, on closer examination every one of its working parts, including us, is inter-dependently connected to all the other working parts. It is, to put it one way, the only truly enclosed ecosystem any of us knows about. To put it another way, it is an organism. It came alive, I shall guess, 3.8 billion years ago today, and I wish it a happy birthday and a long life ahead, for our children and their grandchildren and theirs and theirs.

~ *The Gaia Atlas of Planet Management*[28] ~

Be not afraid to pray – to pray is right.
Pray, if thou canst, with hope; but ever pray,
Though hope be weak, or sick with long delay;
Pray in the darkness, if there be no light.
Far is the time, remote from human sight,
When war and discord on the earth shall cease;
Yet every prayer for universal peace
Avails the blessed time to expedite.

Week 1

Whate'er is good to wish, ask that of Heaven,
Though it be what thou canst not hope to see;
Pray to be perfect, though material leaven
Forbid the Spirit so on earth to be;
But if for any wish thou darest not pray,
Then pray to God to cast that wish away.

~ Hartley Coleridge[29] ~

CONTEMPLATION

If the Son sets you free, you will be free indeed.

~ John 8:36 ~

Sunday

APPROACH

All things work together for good to those who love God.

~ Romans 8:28 ~

PRAISE

1. *From all that dwell below the skies*
   Let the Creator's praise arise:
   Alleluia!
   Let the Creator's name be sung
   Through every land, by every tongue:
   Alleluia!

2. *Eternal are thy mercies, Lord;*
   Eternal truth attends thy word:
   Alleluia!
   Thy praise shall sound from shore to shore,
   Till suns shall rise and set no more:
   Alleluia!

~ Isaac Watts [30] ~

I praise you, Lord for the world into which I was born, for the life that is mine, and for the future that you have prepared for me. You have provided me with a world that bears the traces of your glory; you have given me a life in which I can see you as the Centre; you have opened up for me an eternal life that knows no end.

To you, triune Lord, be praise and honour and blessing and power, world without end, and above all now on this day from my adoring heart.

THANKS

I thank you, Lord, for your universe: for earth and sky, for sun and moon, for stars and light, for plants and shrubs, for birds and fish. I thank you for their sustenance, their variety, their beauty and their design.

I thank you, too, for human beings: for their bodily strength, for their skill and ingenuity of mind, for their ability to dream. Thanks be to you for my life and for that which makes me me.

Week 1

I thank you, Lord, for access to your kingdom and to the spiritual world that lies vibrant within me. I rejoice in the memory of those who have opened my eyes to see the beauty of your world, who have kindled my mind so that I could serve others, who have formed the substance of my dreams, and who have illuminated my inner world. Above all I thank *you*, O Son, for your love reflects human love; I thank *you*, O Spirit, for it is you who dwell within.

In your light, triune God, do I see light. Thank you for all your gifts showered upon me and for the challenge to use them because they are no longer my own but thine. If only I could see this, O Lord!

SELF-EXAMINATION AND FORGIVENESS

1. *How can I stoop to touch your loving feet?*
   My heart is low –
   My gaze forbears your gracious eyes to meet!
   Your mercy show
   To one, distraught, for whom to weep in pain.
   Whence is the balm for me to rise again?

2. *Faint is the cross I see before my eyes –*
   Your mercy show.
   Dull glints the spear in your distorted side!
   Yet it doth glow
   With quivering light, as trembling I arise,
   Bathed in the wounds now ravishing my eyes.

3. *What is this ecstasy of penance now*
   My heart doth know?
   No more to past depression will I bow,
   My joy doth flow!
   Forgiven my sins, in God's hands my life,
   For others I grieve, creative my strife!

MEDITATION

Then Ananias went to the house and entered it. Place his hands on Saul, he said, 'Brother Saul, the Lord Jesus, who appeared to you on the road as you were coming here, has sent me so that you may see again and be filled with the Holy Spirit.' Immediately, something like scales fell from Saul's eyes, and he could see again. He got up and was baptised, and after taking some food, he regained his strength.

~ Acts 9:17–19 ~

Week 1

I have never had an experience like that of Saul on the road to Damascus. Nor, I suppose, have you. I have never been struck blind because of the harm I have done to others. Nor, I dare say, have you. However, I have failed, stumbled and grieved others in small but harmful ways from childhood until now. Perhaps I am emotionally and spiritually blind because there has never been an Ananias to come along and take the scales from my eyes and to say, 'Brother, even in your gaffs and worse, the Lord was there! See again and be filled with the Holy Spirit!'

I – we – go back in imagination into our life's record. We think slowly of each stage of our life, and try to bring to the surface things that happened, things that caused us guilt, or shame, or that were so painful because of what we did (or what we thought we did) that it is hard to look at them or even remember them. We go back to our childhood and to our family relationships – or our lack of them; we go back to our time of education, to what happened to us, and to things that we did at school and college; we go back to our early adult life – to our work situations, and perhaps to our married life. Slowly we look at the blameworthy things we have done, our equivalent of Saul's persecuting the early Christians. Where we feel hurt, and raw, and blameworthy, we repent and say we are sorry. We wake from our blindness about the incident in question, and if necessary we weep. Perhaps Saul wept after he regained his sight from both regret and joy!

We also thank God for bringing them to mind. Indeed, more that that, we thank God for them! If Saul had not set out to persecute the early Christians on the road to Damascus his life might never have been changed! God permitted Saul to persecute the Christians although perhaps he did not will it! It is the same with us. The problem with our regretful deeds is not that we did them (although we cannot be proud of that), but that we did not repent of them, and we did not thank God for the occasion they afforded for him to use them.

Late in time perhaps we express our regret to God now, and we thank him for the good that would have come to us then and that does come to us now. Perhaps this passage is our equivalent to Ananias; perhaps we need to find a local Ananias to complete the work of grace within us.

In wonder lost, perhaps in trembling joy, we realise that everything in our lives – the past we have been reflecting on now, the present day that lies before us, the future that stretches out ahead – is in the hands of God. About our past fall, which might even have been a small thing although of crucial importance to us, we can say (with the church about the fall of Adam, which eventually triggered Christ's cross) *'O felix culpa* – O happy fault' that led to such a wonderful insight. About the future we can dare to agree with St Augustine, who said, 'Love God, and do what you like!' For the scales have fallen from our eyes and we are in the hands of God.

Week 1

PETITION

1. *If choice was given to me, Lord,*
   Of one gift I could take,
   On love, far greater than the sword,
   My entire life I'd stake.

2. *Love's benign tentacles extend*
   The whole world to embrace,
   To count each soul a precious friend
   Of every clime and place.

3. *Till all the seas run dry, O Love,*
   Mid hatred and mid strife,
   You spread your fragrance from above,
   You plead with every life.

4. *And though one person yet remains*
   Beset at planet's end,
   You'll strive with empathetic pain
   A foe to make a friend.

5. *I'll hymn you while I've voice, I'll raise*
   My banner at your call!
   In blessing you it's God I praise,
   My Spur, my Guide, my All!

PRAYER FOR ACTION

The human community is projected to reach at least ten billion before the population explosion fizzles out into zero growth in the twenty-second century.

The problem does not lie only in a sheer outburst of human numbers. It lies also in an outburst of human consumerism. One billion over-affluent people enjoy lifestyles that impose a grossly disproportionate pressure on our planetary ecosystem. This consumerism is powered in turn by a sudden expansion in technological know-how, enabling us to use and misuse ever-greater stocks of natural resources – even to use them up. In fact, rather than a 'population crisis' or a 'resource crisis', we should speak of a single over-arching crisis: the crisis of humankind. The shadow stems from all of us, and it will darken all our lives.

~ The Gaia Atlas of Planet Management [31] *~*

Week 1

Lord, if you have offered your lordship and given me lordship over my own life, it is to impel me to be the servant of all.

Forgive me, Lord, for spiritual individualism. Forgive me for saying the problem is too big and I can't understand it. I know that the starving millions are my brothers and sisters, and your children. I know that faith extends into the whole of life. I know that I am uniquely privileged in so many ways.

Educate me about the global situation. Let me glimpse the deeper meaning of the crisis of humankind. Show me what I can do by writing, by giving, by going, by seeing, by changing my lifestyle. Give me a vision of the new world you would have us to enjoy and give me a part in the miracle of your love, though the very stones cry out!

CONTEMPLATION

Love God, and love your neighbour as yourself.

NOTES

1. From the 'Hebrew Morning Service'. S. Singer (trans.), *Authorised Daily Prayer Book*. See B. Greene and V. Gollancz (eds), *God of a Hundred Names* (London: Gollancz, 1985), p. 259.
2. John Masefield, 'Sonnet XLIV', in *The Collected Poems of John Masefield* (London: Heinemann, 1923), p. 433.
3. Julian of Norwich in Grace Warrack (ed.), *Revelations of Divine Love* (London: Methuen, 1927), p. 52.
4. Fénelon (1651–1715) – see Greene and Gollancz (op. cit.), p. 159.
5. N. Myers (ed.), *The Gaia Atlas of Planet Management* (London and Sydney: Pan Books, 1981), p. 258.
6. Joseph Hart (1712–68) – see *Hymns and Psalms* (London: Methodist Publishing House, 1983), Hymn 277.
7. *Hymns and Psalms* (op. cit.), Hymn 568, verse 1, by Johann Nitschmann (1712–83) and verse 5 by Anna Nitschmann (1715–60) (both trans. John Wesley).
8. St Bonaventure, *The Tree of Life*, in volume on St Bonaventure by E. Cousins (ed.), *Classics of Western Spirituality* (New York: Paulist Press, 1979), pp. 144–5.
9. George Herbert, 'Mary Magdalene', in volume on George Herbert by J. N. Wall (ed.), *Classics of Western Spirituality* (New York: Paulist Press, 1981), p. 299.
10. Adapted from the *Tao te ching*, vii.
11. John Mason (*circa* 1645–94) – see *Hymns and Psalms* (op. cit.), Hymn 8.
12. Poems without reference are by the author of this work.
13. Found in Old St Paul's Church, Baltimore, in 1692.
14. Samuel Taylor Coleridge, 'The Rime of the Ancient Mariner' – see G. Lacey May, arr, *English Religious Verse* (London: Dent, 1937), p. 158.
15. Charles Wesley (1707–88) – see *Hymns and Psalms* (op. cit.), Hymn 501.
16. Julian of Norwich, 'Showings', in volume on Julian of Norwich in the *Classics of Western Spirituality*, pp. 342–3.
17. St Thomas à Kempis, 'The Imitation of Christ' – see *The History of Christianity* (London: Lion Publishing, 1977), p. 356.

Week 1

18. See volume on John and Charles Wesley by Frank Whaling (ed.), *Classics of Western Spirituality* (New York: Paulist Press, 1981), p. 387.
19. Ignatius of Loyola – see *The History of Christianity* (op. cit.), p. 411.
20. Dag Hammarskjold, *Markings* (London: Faber, 1964), p. 127.
21. Richard Baxter (1915–91) – see *Hymns and Psalms* (op. cit.), Hymn 495.
22. *The Collected Poems of John Masefield* (op. cit.), pp. 125, 128.
23. Brother Lawrence, *The Practice of the Presence of God* (London: Epworth Press, n.d.), p. 23.
24. M. Landsberg (trans.) (1845–1928) and Newton Mann (1836–1926), Hymn from the medieval Jewish doxology – see *Hymns and Psalms* (op. cit.), Hymn 56.
25. Abu Bakr (*circa* 572–634) – see Greene and Gollancz (op. cit.), p. 128.
26. George Fox, 'Journal' – see Francis B. James, *For The Quiet Hour* (London: Epworth, 1952), p. 17.
27. William Shakespeare, *Merchant of Venice*, Act IV Scene I – see *Complete Works*, vol. 2, intro by E. Dowden (Frowde London: OUP, 1910), p. 385.
28. N. Myers (ed.), *The Gaia Atlas of Planet Management* (op. cit.), p. 258.
29. Hartley Coleridge (1796–1849) – see G. Lacey May (ed.), *English Religious Verse* (London: Dent, 1937), pp. 174–5.
30. Isaac Watts (1674–1748) – see *Hymns and Psalms* (op. cit.), Hymn 489.
31. N. Myers (ed.), *The Gaia Atlas of Planet Management* (op. cit.), p. 18.

Week 1

Week 2

Monday

APPROACH

Human life, my life, is a sacrosanct miracle.

PRAISE

O God, the parent of our Lord Jesus Christ, and our parent: you who are to us both father and mother: we who are your children draw around your lotus feet to worship you. Your compassion is as the fragrance of the lotus. Though you are enthroned in the heavens, we may draw nigh to you: for your feet stand upon the earth where we humans dwell. Your Son, our Lord, was man.

We see your compassion in Jesus. He gives content to the Hindu name for you – Siva, the Kindly One, the Merciful. He gives significance to the Muslim address for you – Allah, the Merciful. He embodies in the Godhead what the Buddhist worships in the Buddha – compassion itself.

God of all the world, let our history teach us that we belong to you alone and that you alone belong to us. And you are enough, for in you we sinners find sonship and daughterhood again – the one thing that we most need.

~ Adapted from D. T. Niles[1] ~

THANKS

I thank you, Lord, for all the concern you have shown me.

I thank you for the prints of the sacred you have planted in my life, and that in the fullness of time you have unveiled some of the love that you purposed to show forth.

I thank you for your love, which has gone before me all the days of my life, so often unnoticed but always there.

I thank you for the gift of life and personality: for a world of beauty and of challenge in which to develop my life, and for the presence of family and friends with whom to share that life.

I thank you for the gift of faith, which gives pattern to my varied activities, for the gift of love, which makes those activities meaningful, and for the gift of hope, which sets them in the context of your eternity.

I thank you for the gift of yourself: for your fatherhood and majesty which I reverence; for your sonship and saving grace, to which my heart

Week 2

responds with adoring rapture; and for your spiritual indwelling, which echoes as a hunger and a promise within my soul.

When you have spoken often I have not heard, when you have beckoned often I have not followed, when you have gone before often I have not responded, when you have indicated steadfastness often I have gone off on prodigal capers, when you called to daring adventure often I have retreated into passivity, when you were gloriously there often I was too blind to notice – yet I thank you for your strange eternal care for me that seeks and pleads for me, I know not why. And yet I do know, for you are God. Thanks be to you, O merciful and constant Lord!

SELF-EXAMINATION AND FORGIVENESS

Me Lord? Can'st thou mispend
One word, misplace one look on me?
Call'st me thy Love, thy Friend?
Can this poor soul the object be
Of these love-glances, those life-kindling eyes?
What? I the Centre of thy arms' embraces?
Of all thy labour I the prize?
Love never mocks, Truth never lies.
Oh how I quake: Hope fear, fear hope displaces:
I would, but cannot hope: such wondrous love amazes.

~ Phineas Fletcher[2] ~

Your presence and forgiveness are mine, Lord.

When I depart from loving you, loving my neighbour, and loving myself, you are present within me. You have deeper insight into what I do and why I do it than I have. You do not judge me, but by your silent, caring presence you identify with me and I realise that all is not well.

You do not need to say anything, I rebuke myself: in silence you love, it is I who condemn. You love me more than I love myself; you understand me better than I understand myself; you are more aware of me than I am aware of myself; you know me better than I know myself.

For in the silence of your presence, in which I feel condemned, I find mercy and forgiveness. Your presence, in which I feel rebuked, surrounds me with grace and compassion. My tears, which portray sorrow, also show forth joy.

I am forgiven! My heart is melted in your heart. Thank you, Lord!

MEDITATION

I tell you the truth, anyone who has faith in me will do what I have been doing. He will do even greater things than these, because I am going to the Father. And

Week 2

I will do whatever you ask in my name, so that the Son may bring glory to the Father. You may ask me for anything in my name, and I will do it.

~ John 14:12–14 ~

At first sight this passage seems too good to be true. If we have faith in God through Jesus, can we really do what he did? Can we really do greater things than he did? If we ask for anything in his name, will it really be given to us? Will he really do whatever we ask in his name?

If I am honest, for much of the time my answer is probably in the negative. I rationalise my timidity: to do greater things than Jesus would be to diminish him; it was alright for the early Christians but now we live in a scientific age when these things no longer apply; if only I had more faith! But I know in my heart of hearts that these are get-outs. Part of me knows that it is not so much a mental as a moral problem. I don't care enough about the world and the people in it to pray in earnest depth to God on the world's behalf. I am afraid of the implications for me and my lifestyle if the prayers I want to offer were actually answered. I know that to pray like this would involve a change in me that would be far deeper than would be the case if prayer were just a private thing.

What then is the meaning of this passage? How can I take it seriously and put it into practice? What does it mean to pray in the name of Jesus?

Pure Land Buddhists claim that if one of them can say with sincerity the words 'I put my faith in Amida Buddha', this will of itself bring salvation. The crux of the matter lies in the phrase 'with sincerity'. If you or I or other people merely repeat the words 'I put my faith in Amida Buddha' it will effect nothing, because we are not speaking with sincerity. We are offering the parrot-like repetition of a formula. All too often Christian prayer has the words 'in the name of Jesus Christ' tacked on the end as a kind of formula. Of itself it means nothing. It is when it is said with sincerity, 'with faith in Christ' that it becomes meaningful.

In the ancient world, and in the Bible, the word 'name' had a potent force. It meant power or character. Therefore to pray in the name of Jesus meant to pray in the character of Jesus. To pray in the character of Jesus meant to pray in his character, to pray according to his nature, to pray the kind of prayers that he would pray: it meant above all to pray in love. Therefore 'to ask anything' was only part of the equation. It did not mean to ask for someone to die, or to be wafted on a magic carpet from Edinburgh to Vladivostok. To ask anything 'in the name of Jesus' introduced the glorious limitation of love into the equation. Prayer is offered in love and for the sake of love. If I pray out of self-importance or self-contempt, if I pray when tinged by anger, malice, hatred, envy, jealousy or lust, then that prayer is not in love or in the name of Jesus. If I pray for others with indifference to their real concerns, then I am not praying in love or in the name of Jesus or with a desire to share with them the unsearchable riches

Week 2

of God. To pray, then, 'in the name of Jesus' is a high responsibility and a glorious undertaking.

Furthermore, praying in the name of Jesus points beyond both Jesus and ourselves. In one direction the passage points us beyond Jesus to the Father – to whom he is going, to whom he will bring glory, and with whom he is one. Christian prayer is to the Father through Jesus in the Spirit. In another direction it points us to the church. When I pray it is not just a lonely vigil that I pursue in my solitariness, even though I may be alone in my room. My prayer implies other Christians. To pray in the name of Jesus is to pray not just in my own right but as a member of the Body of Christ. Moreover the fellowship of the saints and the church triumphant are praying with me through the spirit even if there is only one physical body in my room! Nor can we rest content with limiting our prayer in the name of Jesus to the Christian community. Prayer in the name of Jesus cannot rest content until it spans (in principle) the whole world. It is to pray in love for the whole earth and its human community.

'O God,' we say, 'the task is too much.' 'No, it is not,' the answer comes. 'Because my Son has come to me and is one with me, the whole church and the whole world is my concern – it is your concern and your parish too. Pray in his name for it, pray in the name of love, and you will do great things. There is nothing more important for you to do, for anyone to do, than to pray in the name of Jesus.'

PETITION

Father, I abandon myself into your hands; do with me what you will. Whatever you may do, I thank you: I am ready for all, I accept all. Let only your will be done in me, and in all your creatures. I wish no more than this, O Lord. Into your hands I commend my soul: I offer it to you with all the love of my heart, for I love you, Lord, and so need to give myself, to surrender myself into your hands, without reserve, and with boundless confidence, for you are my Father.

~ Charles de Foucauld[3] ~

PRAYER FOR ACTION

Ode to Love

1. *Love, the force beyond all others,*
   Shed abroad on planet earth,
   Joining from all creeds and colours
   Those who share in human birth –
   How can we fulfil your promise
   Streaming through the firmament,
   You our challenge and our solace,
   Peace to find, hope to present!

Week 2

2. *Love, redeeming Dream, forever*
   Locked within the human psych',
   Potent is your power to sever
   Loss, to cancel worldly strife!
   May we tap your latent current,
   Harness soon your drive sublime,
   So that on earth there may be sent
   A joy engulfing every clime!

3. *As around the world we wander*
   Soaring high in prayerful gaze,
   Mortal weakness do we ponder,
   Envy, malice, pride and rage;
   Mighty seem their will to stall your
   Plans, your good to bring to nought;
   Mightier still, O Love, your grace, awe,
   Bliss and hope surpassing thought!

4. *Human hearts portray your splendour,*
   Bodies locked in fond embrace
   Fuse in union forged of matter,
   Joy to know, your plot to trace!
   Flesh and blood spurn not your counsel
   Instruments to heed your call,
   Transcend you still their outward spell
   Humane Compassion, Seed of all!

5. *As on eagles' wings we fly to*
   Cry your ecstasy, O Love,
   'Yond the bounds of earth try we to
   See your visage, heavenly Dove!
   Within our soul a voice speaks faint,
   'First seek me here', it says full sweet,
   'My voice, myself, my Me, O saint,
   Within yourself are yet replete!'

6. *In beauteous places do we find*
   You, Love – of beauty You the spur!
   In hovels, dungeons, darkness blind,
   We find You too – nay everywhere
   Where caring hearts respond to need,
   Where empathy claps hands with pain –
   In death's abode, where creatures bleed
   You live, O Love, You there remain!

Week 2

7. *Let not our failures blight our zeal,*
   O Love, your praise to render!
   Forgive our fears, our heartbreak feel,
   You know our wounds so tender!
   So often have we spurned your cross
   Yet, in adoring wonder,
   We give ourselves to You, from loss
   Comes gain, Immortal Lover!

8. *Love, O Love, beyond all rapture,*
   Glorious Love, Radiance divine!
   How can we your secret capture?
   How can we infer your sign?
   'Struggle not,' a voice speaks fondly,
   'Ope your eyes, discern my trail,
   'Tis I seek you, eternally –
   And Love, you know, can never fail!'

Help me, Lord, to love you with heart and mind and strength, and to love my neighbour as myself.

Help me to love you with my heart by responding to you with growing devotion; help me to love you with my mind by directing my intention towards you more constantly; help me to love you with all my strength through the increasing energy of my service.

Help me increasingly to love myself that I may love others better, and to love others better so that I may grow in love towards my developing self. May I rejoice in the comfort of others and sorrow with them in their discomfort. May I greet the welfare and success of others as though it were my own, and sympathise with the tribulations of others as though they had fallen on me.

Grant, Lord, that love of you may lead me to act for others, and that in acting for others I may be led to have a deeper love for you.

CONTEMPLATION

The peace of God, which transcends all understanding,
will guard your hearts and your minds in Christ Jesus.

~ Philippians 4:7 ~

Tuesday

APPROACH

O Lord, you love me unconditionally.

PRAISE

1. *I will exalt you, my God the King; I will praise your name for ever and ever.*
2. *Every day I will praise you and extol your name for ever and ever.*
3. *Great is the Lord and most worthy of praise; his greatness no-one can fathom.*
4. *One generation will commend your works to another; they will tell of your mighty acts.*
5. *They will speak of the glorious splendour of your majesty, and I will meditate on your wonderful works.*
6. *They will tell of the power of your awesome works, and I will proclaim your great deeds.*
7. *They will celebrate your abundant goodness and joyfully sing of your righteousness.*
8. *The Lord is gracious and compassionate, slow to anger and rich in love.*
9. *The Lord is good to all, he has compassion on all he has made.*
10. *All you have made will praise you, O Lord; your saints will extol you.*
11. *They will tell of the glory of your kingdom and speak of your might, so that all men may know of your mighty acts and the glorious splendour of your kingdom.*
12. *Your kingdom is an everlasting kingdom, and your dominion endures through all generations.*
13. *The Lord is faithful to all his promises and loving towards all he has made.*
14. *The Lord upholds all those who fall and lifts up all who are bowed down.*
15. *The eyes of all look to you, and you give them their food at the proper time.*
16. *You open your hand and satisfy the desires of every living thing.*
17. *The Lord is righteous in all his ways and loving towards all he has made.*
18. *The Lord is near to all who call on him, to all who call on him in truth.*
19. *He fulfils the desires of those who fear him; he hears their cry and saves them.*

~ Psalm 145:1–19 ~

I praise you, O Lord, who art small enough to dwell within my tiny frame, yet vast enough to overflow the universe. You are the mighty, stupendous Lord, the King of glory. You are the loving, kind and compassionate Father. You are my Lord, and my God!

For your gentle might, for your amazing grace, for your stooping majesty, for your shepherd heart, for your humble power, I praise you, O Lord, and I love you – and I will do so forever.

Week 2

THANKS

O Lord, I thank you for my times of meeting with you. I thank you for the people through whom I see you. I thank you for the bread and wine through which I receive you. I thank you for the silence through which I hear your footsteps. I thank you for the events through which I sense your traces.

O Lord, meeting is a strange and wonderful thing. How often do I meet people yet not meet them? How often do I take the bread and wine yet am not aware of you? How often do I pray yet have no sense of you? How often am I involved in vibrating happenings yet I don't feel you? How often am I with you and others yet meeting does not take place?

Sensitise me, O Lord, to true meeting. May I have a deeper awareness of the glories of nature and the wonder of human beings because I meet them and am with them with my whole being. Help me to be open to you in prayer that in being met by you I may meet you, and in meeting you my contacts with nature and others may be so transfigured that they become icons of your presence.

Thank you, Lord, for this meeting as I know you with me now.

SELF-EXAMINATION AND FORGIVENESS

Lord, within these walls I see so little beauty; open my eyes.
I find no room or reason in my heart to forgive; open my heart.
I hear the wind in the wire, but not the birds; open my ears.
I smell sweat and fear but not flowers; open my senses.
I do and say nothing about rampant injustice; open my mouth.
Hate is locked tight in the safe of my soul; open me.

Take the bars from my mind and set my spirit free from this prison which I have built with stones of hate.

Free me, Lord; Free me.

~ Prayer of J.B., inmate of Wormwood Scrubs Prison[4] ~

O Lord, grant me the wonder of your forgiveness. In my life:
where there is anxiety, may you bring confidence;
where there is corruption, may you cleanse;
where there is falling, may you restore;
where there is opulence, may you bring simplicity;
where there is arrogance, may you discipline;
where there is a faint heart, may you bestow joy;
where there is lack, may you supply;
where there is faith, hope and love, may you build and deepen.

If we claim to be without sin, we deceive ourselves and the truth is not in us.
If we confess our sins, he is faithful and just and will forgive us our sins and purify us from all unrighteousness.

~ 1 John 1:8–9 ~

Week 2

MEDITATION

Shadrach, Meshach and Abednego replied to the king, 'O Nebuchadnezzar, we do not need to defend ourselves before you in this matter. If we are thrown into the blazing furnace, the God we serve is able to save us from it and he will rescue us from you hand, O king. But even if he does not, we want you to know, O king, that we will not serve your gods or worship the image of gold you have set up.'

~ Daniel 3:16–18 ~

Shadrach, Meshach and Abednego symbolise the Jews at the time of the Maccabees who are threatened with suffering. They symbolise us as well. This short meditation passes through three phases, each of which is important.

The first reaction of Shadrach, Meshach and Abednego to the threat of suffering and persecution is to rebel against it. It is probably our first reaction as well. 'The God we serve is able to save us from it and he will rescue us,' we cry. There is no reason why we should meekly lie down before suffering and persecution and endure them without protest, whether they be inflicted upon us or on others. Prophetic outcry rather than passive acceptance is our first option. God can help and deliver! God may permit our tribulations; he certainly does not will them! By our mental attitude towards our suffering, we can overcome it. Illness can be healed, leprosy can be fought by a Father Damien, the forlorn in the slums of Calcutta can be helped by a Mother Teresa, the blood of the martyrs can become the seed of the church – but we need not become martyrs because the persecution can be stopped!

Then come those fateful words, trivial in themselves, but pregnant with meaning, 'But even if he does not.' Six short words, but how deep in their consequences! What if there is no solution? What if God may not deliver? What if the illness cannot be cured? What if Father Damien gets leprosy himself? What if the persecution cannot be stopped and the church dies out as a result – the blood of the martyrs is not the seed of the church? The blazing furnace is not going to go out and the flames are going to do their worst – what then? 'But even if he does not': six small, unimportant words but how powerful and how poignant! They form the hinge of this passage, and sometimes they form the hinge of our lives. We have fought what we thought was a good fight, and seemingly we have lost.

Shadrach, Meshach and Abednego utter their final, triumphant words and they say, in effect, 'We will be faithful even though the flames prevail!' They reflect Jesus's words in Gethsemane, 'may this cup be taken from me. Yet not as I will, but as you will.' He did not meekly acquiesce in the suffering of the cross at first. If it could be avoided, let it be avoided! Perhaps we Christians often receive suffering and tribulation too readily! Yet when it was clear that it was not to be that God would rescue him from the cross he accepted it gladly. Jesus would be faithful even though the nails prevailed! He surrendered his own death to God and received it back, the same death, but transformed.

Some battles we can and should win. Others, including the final battle with death we cannot win. Yet we too can be faithful even though the flames prevail. And if there are those who scoff, 'Look at all you have done and what has happened to you, yet you have nothing,' we can reply 'The whole hill of Calvary and the fullness of the Risen Lord belong to me!'

PETITION

Lord, I have knelt and tried to pray tonight,
But thy love came upon me like a sleep,
And all desire died out; upon the deep
Of thy mere love I lay, each thought in light
Dissolving like the sunset clouds, at rest
Each tremulous wish and my strength weakness, sweet
As a sick boy with soon o'erwearied feet
Finds, yielding him unto his mother's breast
To weep for weakness there. I could not pray,
But with closed eyes I felt thy bosom's love
Beating toward mine, and then I would not move
Till of itself the joy should pass away;
At last my heart found voice, – 'Take me, O Lord,
And do with me according to thy word.'

~ Edward Dowden[5] ~

PRAYER FOR ACTION

Covenant for Peace of Edinburgh Christian Council

Believing in God the Father, who creates all things, we covenant to care for his world by conserving and sharing the resources of creation.

Believing in God the Son, who reconciles enemies, we covenant to break down barriers between nations and within our own, replacing exploitation with justice, and nuclear weapons with work for peace.

Believing in God the Spirit, who gives life in face of death, we covenant to overcome fear and despair with faith and hope, and to join in initiatives of imagination and courage to effect creative change.

Believing in one church, charged by Jesus Christ to be a sign of God's will and unity, we covenant so to live, that life in its fullness may be open to all humanity.

Week 2

Believing in the Kingdom of God, that is and is coming, we covenant to respond to the love of God in the political reality of his world.

Contentment as Living for Others

Contentment for oneself is only possible when there is prophetic discontent on behalf of others.

Out of true self-love is built effective love for others.

Nuclear power is here forever, so is the humane desire to confine it to creative purposes.

Therefore let us rejoice that we are shed abroad in this cosmos no less than the flowers and the planets – it is our birthright.

Enjoyment includes our aspirations as well as our achievements.

Nothing can separate anyone from the love of God except their acquiescence in separation.

Then let our love and prayer be extended to all.

Meanness divides us from others; love attracts us to others.

Endeavour to practise the presence of God; he is present most often in others.

Never compare, lest arrogance towards others or timidity towards others prevent us from helping them.

Truth is to do with persons rather than statements, with Thous rather than Its.

CONTEMPLATION

Rejoice in the Lord always.

~ Philippians 4:4 ~

Week 2

Wednesday

APPROACH

In him we live, and move, and have our being.

~ Acts 14:28 ~

PRAISE

O God, your greatness surpasses the power of my mind to understand, yet in your humility you wash my feet. I praise you, Lord.

I do not fully know your nature, but I praise you for the world I enjoy.

I do not fully know why I am here, but I praise you for my awareness that I came from you, am with you, and will be with you.

I do not fully know why there is conflict in your world, but I am happy to serve the side of goodness, beauty and truth.

I do not fully appreciate this earth upon which I walk, but I am glad to rejoice in it and watch over it as a steward.

I cannot prove you or analyse you, but I can bless you and love you.

I cannot solve the problem of evil, but I can pray and work for a planet of hope.

There is so much I cannot understand and cannot do, Lord. But this one thing I can do and will do: I can praise you with all my heart.

THANKS

Aristides (about the Early Christians)

> They walk in all humility and kindness, and falsehood is not found among them, and they love one another. They despise not the widow, and grieve not the orphan. He that hath distributeth liberally to him that hath not. If they see a stranger, they bring him under their roof, and rejoice over him as if he were their own brother: for they call themselves brethren, not after the flesh, but after the Spirit of God; but when one of their poor passes away from the world, and any of them see him, then he provides for his burial according to his ability; and if they hear that any of their number is imprisoned or oppressed for the name of their Messiah, all of them provide for his needs, and if it is possible that he

Week 2

may be delivered, they deliver him. And if there is among them a man that is poor and needy, and they have not an abundance of necessaries, they fast two or three days that they may supply the needy with their necessary food.[6]

I thank you, Lord, for this model. Show me what is the equivalent for me in this age, and I will thank you even more.

SELF-EXAMINATION AND FORGIVENESS

Why are you so cast down, my Soul?
Do you not bear the imprints of
Eternity? Can you not soar
Into the cosmos unaware of
Worldly cares? Is not your speed that
Of the wind, your sphere that of the
Flyer unbeset by fog or squall?
Whence this excess of broodingness –
This zeal to hide your true design?

'I cannot void the toils of earth,'
My soul replies, 'to cultivate
Fine airs that mock the roles that flesh
Inherits by my very birth on
This fair orb of pain as well as
Joy, of hope yet sorrow too.
How can you tempt me to betray
What anchors me within the lives
Of those who need me most?'

Dissemble not, O Soul, by sleight
Of thought more specious yet since truth
Is absent not from your embrace.
Earth sure is yours, but heaven is yours
As well. By your conjunction both
Are joined! To abandon the eternal
Is not to gain the globe! Aim high
With trembling joy and see the common
Place aflame with sparks divine!

Forgive me, Lord, my timidity to be valiant for the material and the eternal. Show me how they illuminate each other, that in flying to your bosom I may come closer to the cares of daily life, and in meeting human needs I may be caught up into the seventh heaven.

MEDITATION

Jesus said: 'A man was going down from Jerusalem to Jericho, when he fell into the hands of robbers. They stripped him of his clothes, beat him and went away, leaving his half-dead. A priest happened to be going down the same road, and when he saw the man, he passed by on the other side. So too, a Levite, when he came to the place and saw him, passed by on the other side. But a Samaritan, as he travelled, came where the man was; and when he saw him, he took pity on him. He went to him and bandaged his wounds, pouring on oil and wine. Then he put the man on his own donkey, brought him to an inn and took care of him. The next day he took out two silver coins and gave them to the innkeeper. 'Look after him,' he said, 'and when I return, I will reimburse you for any extra expense you may have.'

~ Luke 10:30–5 ~

I am a refugee – to the world and to myself – or rather I was.

I am a merchant with a consignment of goods to take from Jerusalem to Jericho. The rest of my friends have been waiting for days for a convoy to form. Months ago there were stories of robbers on the road. I can't afford to wait that long. I must be away.

Night has fallen and it is dark. I have lit a fire but it is a little eerie. Was I wise to come alone? Why waste time on such foolish cares? Sleep is pleasant and such is my destination.

I awake with a start. My animal seems to be running away. How can that be? By an instinct I raise my hands to the back of my head, but it is too late to stop blows raining down upon every part of my body. My animal and its goods are gone – can anything be saved? Alas my clothes are being stripped off too.

I have no food, no clothes, no belongings, no medicine for my aching body – and I am all alone. I am a refugee!

Footsteps sound in the dust. I can hardly raise my head to look. Surely help is at hand? The footsteps fade away. It was a priest. The morning is becoming warmer. I hear more footsteps, and this time I have the strength to see who it is. It is a Levite. I smile and groan. A grimace comes on his face and he moves on. The grim truth dawns. I am half-dead, I have nothing, my body looks ugly with the wounds – I am a refugee! O God, what have I done to be so alone and so forlorn in this world!

More footsteps sound. I push myself up to look. As soon as I do so I fall back and pretend to be dead. It is a despised Samaritan! The footsteps come nearer. O God! He stoops down. Ah well, my end has come! What does the future hold anyway? Wonder of strange wonders he picks me up and looks at me, he bandages my wounds, he pours on oil, he pours on wine. I am too wary to register emotion. He brings me on to his own donkey and walks along by the side. We come to an inn. He pays for me and puts me in the innkeeper's hands. Full realisation dawns. I am not alone.

Week 2

Another human being loves me! There is a future to life! I weep and weep.

As I look inside my life I weep as well. Here is the confident part of me, anxious to get ahead, always willing to take risks, debonair, even a little arrogant. Nothing is too difficult to attempt. But this time I have really fallen down – I have put my foot in it with a vengeance! I am ruined and a laughing stock. People pass by on the other side. I am a moral refugee. My life has collapsed and I don't see any future. Parts of myself I thought would help do not. It wasn't altogether my fault but that doesn't seem to matter to them!

Then I see the feminine side of me make an approach. I pretend to be dead for I despise it. I have never taken it seriously, I have repressed it. Wonder of wonders, it picks me up, it bandages my wounds, it pours on oil, it pours on wine, it carries me, it puts me to rest.

O God! Can it be that I don't even know myself? You have given me sources of comfort deep in my own life. Help me to love the refugee in my own life so that everything I do is in harmony. Then when I am whole, send me out to help my brother and sister refugees who may even be more whole than I am but who need my love so much.

PETITION

Lord, how can I help others if I can't help myself? Help me to love myself, every part of myself, then send me out to love my neighbour as myself. For my neighbour is not only the person who needs me, but the person who needs me most.

PRAYER FOR ACTION

As for me, before leaving this planet,
I would like to say this to my human brothers and sisters:
Decide to be a spiritual person
Render others spiritual
Irradiate your spirituality
Treat every moment of your life with divine respect
Love passionately your God-given miraculous life
Be endlessly astonished at your breathtaking consciousness of the universe
Thank God every moment for the tremendous gift of life
Lift your heart to the heavens always
Be a cosmic, divine being, an integral, conscious part of the universe
Contemplate with wonder the miraculous creation all around you
Fill your body, mind, heart and soul with divine trepidation
Know that you are coming from somewhere and that you are going
     somewhere in the universal stream of time

Be always open to the entire universe
Know yourself and the heavens and the earth
Act spiritually
Think spiritually
Love spiritually
Treat every person and living being with humaneness and divine respect
Pray, meditate, practice the art of spiritual living
And be convinced of eternal life and resurrection.

~ Robert Muller[7] ~

CONTEMPLATION

And now these three remain: faith, hope and love.
But the greatest of these is love.

~ 1 Corinthians 13:13 ~

Week 2

Thursday

Your presence is a flame of love, O God.
I lift my heart's candle to the flame.

PRAISE

Praise be to God,
The Cherisher and sustainer of the worlds;

Most gracious, most merciful;
Master of the Day of Judgment.

Thee do we worship,
And thine aid we seek.

Show us the straight way,
The way of those on whom
Thou hast bestowed thy grace.

~ Koran 1[8] ~

O Lord, I give you the praise of my heart. I sit alone in my room yet I am aware that my praise is joined with that of others in heaven and on earth. Holy, holy, holy, Lord God Almighty, heaven and earth are full of your glory; glory be to you, O Lord most high! Blessed by you, O Lord, the great I am, whom angels do admire!

I praise you too for the still small silence of your presence. I bless you that you condescend to be close to me. In truth I know that you have never left me. I praise you that though you are everywhere and fill all things you become illumined in the silence of my heart. I praise you that you light up your kingdom within. I praise you for the presence of your grace, and to your name be the glory, now and forever.

THANKS

And in this he showed me something small, no bigger than a hazelnut, lying in the palm of my hand, as it seemed to me, and it was as round as a ball. I looked at it with the eye of my understanding and thought: What can this be? I was

Week 2

amazed that it could last, for I thought that because of its littleness it would suddenly have fallen into nothing. And I was answered in my understanding: It lasts and always will, because God loves it; and thus everything has being through the love of God.

In this little thing I saw three properties. The first is that God made it, the second is that God loves it, the third is that God preserves it. But what did I see in it? It is that God is the Creator and the protector and the lover. For until I am substantially united to him, I can never have perfect rest or true happiness, until, that is, I am so attached to him that there can be no created thing between my God and me.

~ Julian of Norwich[9] ~

I thank you, O God, that you have given me life and set me down on earth at this time and in this place. I thank you for your protecting power in the various trails of my life. I thank you for your love which has prompted me when I have forgotten you, reclaimed me when I have deserted you, and which pleads with me now in the cavern of my being. I thank you for your call to me to be so attached to you, weak as I am, that there can be no created thing between my God and me. Can it be, O Lord, that the frontiers between heaven and earth are collapsed even in this study? I thank you, Lord, that your kingdom has begun on earth as it is in heaven.

SELF-EXAMINATION AND FORGIVENESS

1. *Come, O thou Traveller unknown,*
   Whom still I hold, but cannot see!
   My company before is gone,
   And I am left alone with thee;
   With thee all night I mean to stay,
   And wrestle till the break of day.

2. *In vain thou strugglest to get free,*
   I never will unloose my hold;
   Art thou the Man that died for me?
   The secret of thy love unfold:
   Wrestling, I will not let thee go
   Till I thy name, thy nature know.

3. *Yield to me now – for I am weak,*
   But confident in self-despair!
   Speak to my heart, in blessings speak,
   Be conquered by my instant prayer:
   Speak, or thou never hence shalt move,
   And tell me if thy name is LOVE.

4. *'Tis Love! 'Tis Love! Thou diedst for me;*
   I hear thy whisper in my heart,
   The morning breaks, the shadows flee,
   Pure Universal Love thou art:
   To me, to all, thy mercies move –
   Thy nature, and thy name, is LOVE.

~ Charles Wesley[10] ~

MEDITATION

So Jacob was left alone, and a man wrestled with him till daybreak. When the man saw that he could not overpower him. He touched the socket of Jacob's hip so that his hip was wrenched as he wrestled with the man. Then the man said, 'Let me go, for it is daybreak'.

But Jacob replied, 'I will not let you go unless you bless me'.

The man asked him, 'What is your name?'

'Jacob', he answered.

Then the man said, 'Your name will no longer be Jacob, but Israel, because you have struggled with God and with men and have overcome'.

Jacob said, 'Please tell me your name'.

But he replied, 'Why do you ask my name?' Then he blessed him there.

So Jacob called the place Peniel, saying, 'It is because I saw God face to face, and yet my life was spared.

~ Genesis 32:24–32 ~

Jacob is alone at night facing a crossroads in his life. He is obeying a call to return to Esau, the brother whom he had wronged. For all he knows tomorrow will bring death at the hands of Esau. It is a thought-provoking, numinous time in his life. At times like this the past passes before the screen of the imagination at great speed. In Jacob's case, the past has its skeletons. He reflects on how he had tricked his brother Esau into selling his birthright for food at a time of hunger; he reflects on how he had cheated his father by wearing a coat of skin to pretend he was Esau. He remembers too his flight from Esau, his suffering, his encounter with God, his love for Rachel – yet they serve only to assuage not to obliterate his early treacheries. Past shame, future uncertainty – such are the backcloths to Jacob's present experience.

At times in our lives, you and I are Jacob. Past failures may have been forgiven, they may even have been used, and integrated into more creative living. But their implications, both good and bad, for the future are not yet exhausted. A climactic experience lies ahead. And its outcome and meaning are not certain.

Jacob's struggle seems to be a combination of spiritual wrestling and a dream. He wrestles with a spiritual power, 'a man', and the wrestle takes place at night – daybreak will see its retirement. The power wounds him

Week 2

in the hip. Jacob must have been tempted to retreat from the spot at great pace. Aloneness, the darkness, the numinous atmosphere, this strange adversary were prime ingredients for retreat. And indeed spiritual experience does 'wrench our hip', it does wound us, and our temptation is to avoid it or minimise it.

In spite of his past shortcomings, Jacob is a man of spiritual courage. In the end it is the adversary who begs for mercy, and the chance to go. But Jacob presses on. He had not struggled throughout the night in the throes of this experience in order to miss its meaning right at the end. He wants a blessing. Jacob is asked his name, and when he says it is Jacob the man replies that now he has a new name – Israel – the one who has striven with God.

Names were (and are) of crucial importance. We see this when Jacob asks the stranger his name. He refuses to give it. The stranger, God, has wrestled with Jacob, who has seen God and lived. But he is not ready to know the name, the essence, of God. It would be too much for him. Only Moses had been equal to that. Jacob has gained from this spiritual battle, this wrestling with God, but he still has further to go along life's journey even after he has been reconciled with Esau.

Like Jacob we are tempted to draw back from the numinous experience that can give us a slight wound as well as lead us on to greater awareness. We too are tempted to avoid or minimise these climactic periods and therefore miss our providential hour.

The bravery to engage in spiritual wrestling, the courage to respond to the call of God are potent weapons in the spiritual armoury. Wrestling with God is often a wrestling with ourselves at the prompting of God. Yet it has its times and its seasons. Jacob 'saw God and lived' but he was ready to know the name of God. God does not lead us into temptation that is too great to bear, but he does test us within the limits of our present growth to the end that we may press ever onwards to be the people that he wants us to be.

PETITION

Lord, save us from saying that someone else stands in the way of our growth into your freedom. Help us to see that so often we do not really want the encounters that would wound as well as heal us. It is not that others are preventing our development, we are doing it ourselves.

Grant, O Lord, that when your time comes we may be ready even to wrestle with you that your will may be done.

From Unreality lead me to Reality.
From Darkness lead me to Enlightenment.
From Death lead me to Immortality.

~ Brihadaranyaka Upanishad[11] ~

PRAYERS FOR ACTION

1. *Stay, Master, stay upon this heavenly hill:*
   A little longer, let us linger still;
   With all the mighty ones of old beside,
   Near to the awful Presence still abide;
   Before the throne of light we trembling stand,
   And catch a glimpse into the spirit-land.

2. *Stay, Master, stay! We breathe a purer air;*
   This life is not the life that waits us there:
   Thoughts, feelings, flashes, glimpses come and go;
   We cannot speak them – nay, we do not know;
   Wrapt in this cloud of light we seem to be
   The thing we fain would grow – eternally.

3. *No, saith the Lord, the hour is past, we go;*
   Our home, our life, our duties lie below.
   While here we kneel upon the mount of prayer,
   The plough lies waiting in the furrow there.
   Here we sought God that we might know his will;
   There we must do it, serve him, seek him still.

4. *If man aspires to reach the throne of God,*
   O'er the dull plains of earth must lie the road:
   He who best does his lowly duty here,
   Shall mount the highest in a nobler sphere:
   At God's own feet our spirits seek their rest,
   And he is nearest him who serves him best.

~ Samuel Greg [12] ~

CONTEMPLATION

I know that my Redeemer liveth.

~ Job 19:25 ~

Week 2

Friday

APPROACH

Speak, Lord, for your servant is listening.

~ 1 Samuel 3:9 ~

PRAISE

You are God and we praise you:
you are the Lord and we acclaim you;
You are the eternal Father:
all creation worships you.
To you all angels, all the powers of heaven:
cherubim and seraphim sing in endless praise,
Holy, holy, holy, Lord God of power and might,
heaven and earth are full of your glory.
The glorious company of apostles praise you:
the noble fellowship of prophets praise you,
the white-robed army of martyrs praise you.
Throughout the world the holy Church acclaims you:
Father of majesty unbounded.
Day by day we bless you:
we praise your name for ever.

~ *Te Deum* 1–6, 15 ~

THANKS

I thank you, Lord, for the gift of this day. It is your gift and my privilege.

I thank you for the gift of Christ: for his humility of conduct, for his concern for the suffering, for his inward authority, for his non-violent kingdom, for his manner of love.

I thank you that as Christ abides in me, he desires his bearing to abide in me as well.

I thank you for all my fellow humans who are striving to create a new world for the age in which we live.

I thank you for those who are seeking for international peace.

I thank you for those who are striving for justice especially in conditions where it is hard to do this.

Week 2

I thank you for those who are seeking to relieve famine.

I thank you for those who have it in their hearts and within their power to work for an end to poverty.

I thank you for those occupied in the healing and prevention of disease.

I thank you for those seeking to oppose tyranny, cruelty and man-made distress.

I thank you for those working to research creative and wholesome uses for genetics, electronics and nuclear power.

I thank you for those who are creating bridges between different cultures, religions and world-views.

I thank you for those who are seeking to realise a vision of our coming global world as one of diversity, harmony and creativity.

I thank you, Lord, that had you been alive you would have wanted to do this, and that by abiding in us you can and will do this.

SELF-EXAMINATION AND FORGIVENESS

Forgive us, Lord, we acknowledge ourselves as type of the common man,
Of the men and women who shut the door and sit by the fire;
Who fear the blessing of God, the loneliness of the night of God, the
*   surrender required, the deprivation inflicted;*
Who fear the injustice of men less than the justice of God;
Who fear the hand at the window, the fire in the thatch, the fist in the tavern,
*   the push into the canal,*
Less than we fear the love of God.
We acknowledge our trespass, our weakness, our fault; we acknowledge
That the sin of the world is upon our heads; that the blood of the martyrs
*   and the agony of the saints*
Is upon our heads.
Lord, have mercy upon us.

~ T. S. Eliot[13] ~

MEDITATION

I am the true vine, and my Father is the gardener. He cuts off every branch in me that bears no fruit, while every branch that does bear fruit he prunes so that it will be even more fruitful. You are already clean because of the word I have spoken to you. Remain in me, and I will remain in you. No branch can bear fruit by itself; it must remain in the vine. Neither can you bear fruit unless you remain in me.

I am the vine; you are the branches. If a man remains in me and I in him, he will bear much fruit; apart from me you can do nothing. If anyone does not remain in me, he is like a branch that is thrown away and withers; such branches are picked up, thrown into the fire and burned. If you remain in me and my words remain in you, ask whatever you wish, and it will be given you. This is my Father's glory, that you bear much fruit, showing yourselves to be my disciples.

~ John 15:1–8 ~

Week 2

I pause to pass through into the inner room of my soul. I enjoy its silence and peace. I gaze at its contours: the doors, the windows, the floor, the ceiling; but above all I rest within its calm and quiet. I realise the presence of Christ there and I relax into it.

I see a door at one end of the room. I get up and pass through it. It leads out into a garden. I walk into the garden and enjoy its beauty. I recall the most beautiful garden I have ever seen. It is like that garden, and I walk around it. I see the flowers, the grass, the trees, the water, the colours. I pause in front of a huge vine. I look at it closely: its stem, its branches, its tendrils, its clusters of fruit. I try to merge into a branch of the vine, but somehow I can't. It doesn't work. I look up and see that Christ is beside me. 'Never mind,' he says. 'You don't have to merge into it, you have to meditate on it and learn from it.' So I try.

I see that the vine is present in all its parts: in the stem, the branches, the tendrils, the clusters. I see Christ present in my being, not just in the inner room and garden of my heart. I feel his presence coursing through my veins, my muscles, my head, my chest, my arms, my legs, my feet. I am not trying to prise Christ's present out of him, as though he were a vine separate from its branches. He is already in me and it is up to me to realise it. He abides in me as a patient and often hidden guest. Am I willing to abide in him? If so, I can appreciate to the full his abiding in me.

I see that some parts of the vine are hanging loose, snapping off, decaying, unproductive. I look into the different parts of my life. I review as calmly and dispassionately as possible the state of my body, the state of my mind, the state of my spiritual life. I look at my relationships at home, at work, at large. I look at my effectiveness in the different spheres of my life. Does anything need cutting out or changing? If so what, and how will I do it?

I see the clusters of fruit and notice that the branches are strong where the fruit is found, and they are strongly moulded within the vine. The vine and the branch are one. The first is in the second and the second is in the first. I remember the saying, 'It is no longer I that live but Christ that lives within me,' and another saying, 'For me to live is Christ'. Does then Christ think in me, see in me, speak in me, love in me? I swallow hard. The answer is sometimes, perhaps rarely. How much freer, lighter and more fruitful life would be if the ratio changed, and it was not all my effort, my striving, my seeing, my loving but his effort, his striving, his seeing, his loving.

Christ is still with me in the garden looking at the vine. He says, 'Remain in me, and I will remain in you.'

Week 2

PETITION

1. *O heavenly vine*
     Within me abide!
   O succour divine
     In my heart preside!
   Your life mine transforming,
     So patient and kind,
   Your joy mine enriching,
     In my soul I find!

2. *A garden is formed*
     Within me how deep,
   Its fragrance profound
     Enriches my sleep!
   Of mortals the Being,
     So faithful and true,
   O Gardener all-seeing,
     My being renew!

3. *Your life within me*
     I daily discern,
   But O may I see
     A fruitful return!
   Resources o'erflowing
     Release in me now
   Seed-giving Redeemer,
     My indwelling Thou!

4. *Lone branches thrive not*
     In this your world-tree,
   Connected throughout
     In you we hang free!
   Each other refining
     In you may we dwell,
   The whole world sustaining,
     O life-giving Well!

5. *My burgeoning buds,*
     O may you unfurl,
   Sustaining my roots,
     To answer your call!
   That persons torn, twisted,
     Neglected and low,
   In me may find nurture
     Through your surging flow.

Week 2

6. *So let me abide*
   In you, gracious Lord!
   My indwelling Vine!
   My spiritual sword
   To sever my knots
   To fight hatred and wrong!
   My blessed Communion!
   My immanent Song!

PRAYERS FOR ACTION

God be in my head, and in my understanding;
God be in my eyes, and in my looking;
God be in my mouth, and in my speaking;
God be in my heart, and in my thinking;
God be at mine end, and at my departing.

~ Book of Hours[14] ~

An Affirmation of Global Peace

I see a world in which there is a global commonwealth, with war having no legitimacy anywhere. There is universal support of appropriate peacekeeping institutions. Each of earth's citizens has a reasonable chance to create, through his or her own efforts, a decent life for self and family. Men and women live in harmony with earth and its creatures, co-operating to create and maintain a wholesome environment for all. There is, around the globe, an ecology of different cultures, the diversity of which is appreciated and supported. Throughout, there is a deep and shared sense of meaning in life itself.

CONTEMPLATION

Freely you have received, freely give.

~ Matthew 10:8 ~

Week 2

Saturday

Be still and know that I am God.

~ Psalm 46:10 ~

PRAISE

St Francis's 'Canticle of Brother Sun'

1. *Most High, all-powerful, good Lord,*
   Yours are the praises, the glory, the honour, and all blessing,
2. *To You alone, Most High, do they belong,*
   and no man is worthy to mention Your name.
3. *Praised by You, my Lord, with all your creatures,*
   especially Sir Brother Sun,
   Who is the day and through whom You give us light.
4. *And he is beautiful and radiant with great splendour;*
   and bears a likeness of You, Most High One.
5. *Praised by You, my Lord, through Sister Moon and the stars,*
   in heaven You formed them clear and precious and beautiful.
6. *Praised by You, my Lord, through Brother Wind,*
   and through the air, cloudy and serene, and every kind of weather
   through which You give sustenance to Your creatures.
7. *Praised be You, my Lord, through Sister Water,*
   which is very useful and humble and precious and chaste.
8. *Praised be You, my Lord, through Brother Fire,*
   through whom You light the night
   and he is beautiful and playful and robust and strong.
9. *Praised be You, my Lord, through our Sister Mother Earth,*
   who sustains and governs us,
   and who produces varied fruits with coloured flowers and herbs.
10. *Praised be You, my Lord,*
    through those who give pardon for Your love
    and bear infirmity and tribulation.
11. *Blessed are those who endure in peace*
    for by You, Most High, they shall be crowned.

Week 2

12. *Praised be You, my Lord, through our Sister Bodily Death,*
     from whom no living man can escape.
13. *Praise and bless my Lord and give Him thanks*
     and serve Him with great humility.[15]

THANKS

I thank you, Lord, for the beauty seen in your creation. I thank you for the sun that lights my day, and the moon that guides me by night. I thank you for the heavens above, and the earth below. I thank you for the heat of fire, the moistness of water, and the rush of the mighty wind. I thank you for flowers, and birds, and hills. I thank you for the Grand Canyon, and the Himalayas, and for other things of beauty that fill my heart with joy.

In their beauty I see you, who art Beauty. The handiworks of your creation fill me with awe. I thank you for them, for in them I see a ladder leading from earth into the fullness of your being.

The earth is the Lord's and everything in it;
the world, and all who live in it;
for he hath founded it upon the seas and established it upon the waters.
Who may ascend the hill of the Lord?
Who may stand in his holy place?
He who has clean hands and a pure heart,
who does not lift up his soul to an idol or swear by what is false.
He will receive blessing from the Lord
and vindication from God his Saviour.
Such is the generation of those who seek him,
who seek your face, O God of Jacob.
Lift up your heads, O you gates:
be lifted up, you ancient doors,
that the King of glory may come in.
Who is this King of glory?
The Lord strong and mighty, the Lord mighty in battle.
Lift up your heads, O you gates:
lift them up, you ancient doors,
that the King of glory may come in.
Who is he, this King of glory?
The Lord Almighty – he is the King of glory.

~ Psalm 24 ~

SELF-EXAMINATION

What is this spur, this barb that
Thrusts, with wounding force upon the
Tranquil tenor of my life? Whence to

Week 2

Me, O Lord, this lance of pain
That glows with fire within the
Quivering membranes of my breast?
Why this excess of testing?
Answer me, O Lord, for you
Have said that trials too severe
Should not be borne.

Perchance it is my shadow
Probing, like an angel,
Deep into the secrets hid
With skill from you and humans
But yet alas not from myself.
Or else is it your Spirit
Saying: Wake! Your slumber
Has interfered too long with
What I have in mind for you!

Rejoice! The piercing cries out
Growth, and hope, and depth, and love.
How else, O Lord, can I go
On? Weakness is power, distress
Is joy, at any rate as seen
Within the vision, that is
Yours of where I am. The test
Is but a symbol of your love
That never, never lets me go.

Who shall separate us from the love of Christ? Shall trouble or hardship or persecution or famine or nakedness or danger or sword?

No, in all these things we are more than conquerors through him who loved us.

For I am convinced that neither death nor life, neither angels nor demons, neither the present nor the future, nor any powers, neither height nor depth, nor anything else in all creation, will be able to separate us from the love of God that is in Christ Jesus our Lord.

~ Romans 8:35–9 ~

MEDITATION

Ten Commandments for Earth Caring

1. I am the Lord your God who has created the heavens and the earth. Know that you are my partners in creation. Therefore take care of air, water, earth, plants and animals as if they were your brothers and sisters.
2. Know that in giving you life I have given you responsibility, freedom and limited resources.

Week 2

3. Steal not from the future; honour your children by giving them a chance of longevity.
4. Implant in your children a love of nature.
5. Remember that humanity can use technology but cannot re-create life that has been destroyed.
6. Set up pressure groups within your community to prevent impending catastrophes.
7. Throw out all arms which cause irreversible destruction to the foundations of life.
8. Be self-disciplined in the small details of your life.
9. Set aside time in your weekly day of rest to be with the world rather than to use the world.
10. Remember that you are not the owner of the land merely its guardian.

Every part of the earth is sacred – the leaves of the trees – the sand upon the shore – every mist in the dark woods, every humming insect is holy in the memory and experience of our race.

This beautiful earth is our mother. We are part of the earth, and the earth is part of us. The perfumed flowers are our sisters; the deer, the horse, the peacock our brothers. This shining water which moves in the streams and rivers is not just water, but the blood of our ancestors.

The air is precious, for all things share the same breath. The word that gave our grandparents their first breath also receives their last sigh. You must keep the earth sacred and clean so that we can taste the wind sweetened by the meadows' flowers.

Without animals and plants, rivers and birds, people would die from great loneliness of spirit. For whatever happens to the land and animals soon overtakes man himself. If men spit on the ground, they spit on themselves.

The earth does not belong to us, we belong to the earth. All things are connected, like the blood which animates our frames. Man did not weave the web of life; he is merely a strand in it. Whatever he does to the web he does to himself.

~ Testimony by Chief Seattle[16] ~

Therefore I tell you, do not worry about your life, what you will eat or drink; or about your body, what you will wear. Is not life more important than food, and the body more important than clothes? Look at the birds of the air; they do not sow or reap or store away in barns, and yet your heavenly Father feeds them. Are you not much more valuable than they? Who of you by worrying can add a single hour to his life?

And why worry about clothes? See how the lilies of the field grow. They do not labour or spin. Yet I tell you that not even Solomon in all his splendour was dressed like one of these. If that is how God clothes the grass of the field, which is here today and tomorrow is thrown into the fire, will he not much more clothe you, O you of little faith? So do not worry, saying, 'What shall we eat?' or 'What shall we drink?' or 'What shall we wear?' For the pagans run after all these things, and your heavenly Father knows that you need them. But seek first his kingdom and his righteousness, and all these things will be given to you as well.

Week 2

Therefore do not worry about tomorrow, for tomorrow will worry about itself. Each day has enough trouble of its own.

~ Matthew 6:25–34 ~

PETITION

1. *Lord, bring the day to pass*
     When forest, rock and hill,
   The beasts, the birds, the grass,
     Will know your finished will:
   When we attain our destiny,
   And nature its lost unity.

2. *Forgive our careless use*
     Of water, ore and soil –
   The plenty we abuse
     Supplied by others' toil:
   Save us from making self our creed;
   Turn us towards our neighbour's need.

3. *Give us, when we release*
     Creation's secret powers,
   To harness them for peace –
     Our children's peace and ours:
   Teach us the art of mastering,
   Which makes life rich, and draws death's sting.

4. *Creation groans, travails,*
     Estranged its present plight,
   Bound – till the hour it hails
     The children of the light
   Who enter on their true estate.
   Come, Lord: new heavens and earth create.

~ Ian M. Fraser [17] ~

PRAYER

O Lord, you loved this earth enough to become flesh upon its surface. Help me to love it too. Not as a thing to be used, not as a thing at all, but as my fellow in your creation, and as that over which you have placed me as steward.

I thank you for its beauty. I thank you for its unseen powers. I thank you for its acceptance of me into its bosom. I thank you for the service it gives to me in so many ways.

Week 2

Forgive me, O Lord, for my part in polluting it, for my part in devaluing it. You said, 'This earth is the Lord's and the fullness thereof.' I thought it was mine to use and to forget. Forgive me, O Lord.

I pray for a vision of the world within the compass of your love: a world alive not dead; a world that supplies all the human family with food; a world whose resources are shared by all; a world on whose surface all races live in harmony; a world whose hidden beauties point to the Beloved; a world of vibrant joy for all the human race.

Help me to live in peace and sympathetic love in this part of your garden, O Lord, where I am placed. And in coming closer to you, O Sister Earth, may I come closer to the One who made us both to love and enjoy and serve one another.

CONTEMPLATION

O Lord, our Lord, how majestic is your name in all the earth!

~ Psalm 8:1 ~

Sunday

The Lord is good to all; he has compassion on all he has made.

~ Psalm 145:9 ~

PRAISE

I place before my inward eyes my self with all that I am – my body, soul, and all my powers – and I gather round me all the creatures which God ever created in heaven, on earth, and in all the elements, each one severally with its name, whether birds of the air, beasts of the forest, fishes of the water, leaves and grass of the earth, or the innumerable sand of the sea, and to these I add all the little specks of dust which glance in the sunbeams, with all the little drops of water which ever fell or are falling from dew, snow, or rain, and I wish that each of these had a sweetly sounding stringed instrument, fashioned from my heart's inmost blood, striking on which they might each send up to our dear and gentle God a new and lofty strain of praise for ever and ever. And then the loving arms of my soul stretch out and extend themselves towards the innumerable multitude of all creatures, and my intention is, just as a free and blithesome leader of a choir stirs up the singers of his company, even so to turn them all to good account by inciting them to sing joyously, and to offer up their hearts to God. 'Sursum corda.'

~ Heinrich Suso[18] ~

THANKS

I thank you, Lord, for the exciting and disturbing world of today, for the reality of this day, for the reality of my life this day, and for your reality in my life today.

I thank you for the fun and the joy – and the danger – of this day with its impending ebbs and flows, for the possibility of contributing something new and genuine, and even for the possibility of going wrong.

I thank you for the opportunities that will come to see the viewpoint of others, to get inside their view of the world, to mourn with the mourner and rejoice with the glad.

I thank you for the freedom of this day – from fear, from exhaustion, from being unable to communicate, from craving recognition.

Week 2

I thank you for the chance to talk and the chance to be quiet, for the opportunity to listen and the opportunity to speak, for the routine that I can anticipate and for the purposes that will make all new.

I thank you for the mysterious gift of life, my life, your life, and the life of all my fellows. Bless my life this day for your sake and for their sakes.

SELF-EXAMINATION AND FORGIVENESS

Master of existence, and Lord of lords, we do not rely on our own good deeds but on your great mercy as we lay our needs before you. Lord, hear! Lord, pardon! Lord, listen and act! What are we? What is our life? What is our love? What is our justice? What is our success? What is our endurance? What is our power? Lord our God, and God of our ancestors, what can we say before you, for in your existence are not the powerful as nothing, the famous as if they had never existed, the learned as if without knowledge, and the intelligent as if without insight. To you most of our actions are pointless and our daily life is shallow. Even the superiority of human beings over the beasts is nothing. For everything is trivial except the pure soul which must one day give its account and reckoning before the judgement seat of your glory.

~ Reform Synagogue Sabbath Morning Service ~

1. *Oft I in my heart have said,*
    Who shall ascend on high?
   Mount to Christ my glorious head,
    And bring him from the sky?
   Borne on contemplation's wing,
    Surely I should find him there,
   Where the angels praise their King,
    And gain the morning star.

2. *Oft I in my heart have said,*
    Who to the deep shall stoop?
   Sink with Christ among the dead,
    From thence to bring him up?
   Could I but my heart prepare,
    By unfeigned humility,
   Christ would quickly enter there,
    And ever dwell with me.

3. *But the righteousness of faith*
    Hath taught me better things:
   'Inward turn thine eyes' (it saith,
    While Christ to me it brings),

Week 2

'Christ is ready to impart
Life to all for like who sigh;
In thy mouth, and in thy heart,
The word is ever nigh.'

~ Charles Wesley [19] ~

I will arise and to my Father go;
This very hour the journey is begun.
I start to reach the blissful goal, and, lo,
My spirit at one bound her race has run.
For seeking God and finding Him are one,
He feeds the rillets that towards Him flow.
It is the Father Who first seeks the son,
And moves all heavenward movement, swift or slow.
I dare not pride myself on finding Him.
I dare not dream a single step was mine.
His was the vigour in the palsied limb –
His the electric fire along the line –
When drowning, His the untaught power to swim,
Float o'er the surge, and grasp the rock divine.

~ John Charles Earle [20] ~

MEDITATION

This, then, is how you should pray: Our Father in heaven, hallowed be your name, your kingdom come, your will be done on earth as it is in heaven. Give us today our daily bread. Forgive us our debts, as we also have forgiven our debtors. And lead us not into temptation, but deliver us from the evil one.

~ Matthew 6:9–13 ~

I am quiet before God. I hear my heart beat; I become aware of my breath. As I breathe in, I breathe in God's life into my being; as I breathe out I breathe out the negative things I am aware of. I settle down into a rhythm. I pass through the inner chamber of my heart, and I meditate again on these familiar words, the Lord's Prayer.

'Our Father': I rejoice that I can call you Abba, Father, but you are our Father, the Father of all: of the people of all races, colours, and continents – of Hindus, Buddhists, Muslims, Jews, Marxists and Humanists – of young and old, rich and poor, men and women. When I say 'we', it can no longer be confined to 'we Christians', 'we westerners', or 'we members of any in group'. You are the Father of us all; 'we' are the human race. If I am to honour you as Father I must also honour my fellows whose Father you are. But I am so unworthy, Father, for such a mighty task!

Week 2

'Your kingdom come': I long for your kingdom to grow within me, Father; but surely your kingdom is not just an individual thing to do with me and you, with my spirit and your spirit: it involves people in community and in fellowship, in principle it involves the whole human race in community and in fellowship. But this is so deep a thought and so deep a task, Father!

'On earth as it is in heaven': do you really mean the whole earth – with its racial discrimination, with its sexual inequality, with its divide between the rich north and the poor south, with its political divide between the great powers, with its seeming inhumanity; do you really mean the earth itself – where pollution is spreading, where nuclear holocaust threatens, where species are being slaughtered, where ecological disaster beckons? Are you trying to blow my mind, Father?

'Our daily bread': I am deeply grateful for my daily provision, Father: but the Lord's Prayer speaks of our daily bread, it conjures up a vision of daily provision of the needs of the whole human family. Yet a third of the world's children go to bed each night without having received their daily bread; hundreds of millions have no real home to call their own. I ask for material bread – and mental and spiritual bread – for all, but I do so in agony and trembling.

'Forgive us our debts, as we also have forgiven our debtors': there you go again, Father, it is not just me being forgiven by you and me forgiving other people, it is praying for a general increase of forgiveness among all peoples. How I long for it, and how hard it seems!

'Lead us not into temptation, but deliver us from evil': not just 'me', but 'us' again: our meaninglessness, our spiritual malaise, our egotism, our distorted values. I am coming to realise that I cannot really say this as an individual prayer. I can only pray these things for myself if I am willing to pray them for all of us. I have come into this room alone with you in order to engage with your human family on earth. Who is sufficient for this – for this revolution? I know I am not, Father. 'My child, it is my kingdom, my power and my glory not yours. You are not alone, you are part of my family one earth. You are not alone now. I will always be with you.'

PETITION

Lord, help me to think clearly, to feel deeply, and to pray earnestly about the things I have been meditating upon. Save me from the unhelpful humility of supposing that the task is too big and that there is nothing I can do. Your work may be accomplished without me, but your constraint is laid upon me.

Help me to seek out the facts about our global family. Help me to have an intelligent concern for those in need, and a willingness to become involved in public policy and social concern on their behalf.

Week 2

Help me to pray more sensitively to be drawn closer to the needs of my brothers and sisters, and as I am drawn closer to your wider family may I delight more in the sweetness of your presence – for you are the Father of us all.

INTERCESSION

Ode to Beauty

1. *Therefore your praise with joy to sing*
   We come, O Beauty, muse divine –
   How can we hymn you, confessing
   Our inner blindness to the sign
   That daily to our wandering eyes
   Beams forth your radiance, shining long,
   Sending, for our awakening, spies
   To prompt our hearts to rising song.

2. *The skies above, your clouds do trail*
   Of soaring line and wondrous light;
   The earth below responds, her tale
   Of hills and falls, cascading sight!
   On eagles' wings, on hooves of deer,
   Creatures show forth your form sublime;
   In surging seas the fish appear
   Your grace to show, your tune to rhyme.

3. *O grant us strength that outward scenes*
   May rouse within us echoing chords
   Of archetypal rhythms deep
   Awhile forgot, yet pricking swords
   To stir our conscience from its rest,
   To heal the split 'twixt eye and soul,
   That far inside a vision blest
   May form of You, who makest whole!

4. *Keep silent not, O spirit mine,*
   Of what in you is taking birth –
   My mind leaps up, reflecting fine
   The growing bliss of inner mirth
   Inflaming, surging, soaring long,
   Refining dross, unfolding awe –
   Ah! Now I know! 'Tis beauty strong
   Crying, 'I live right at your core!'

Week 2

5. *I need not now my gaze cast wide*
   O'er sky and earth to own your sway.
   You live within! I cannot hide
   From you like night can hide from day!
   Yet through your clasp, encircling light,
   When outward still my eyes do turn
   Grass, firmament, and all in sight
   With incandescent light do burn!

6. *Beauty, glorious boon, for ever*
   Showered forth on planet earth.
   How shall we, through our endeavour,
   Serve your cause, extol your worth?
   Painting, sculpture, music, writing
   Own your merits, dance your lay,
   Grant that we, our lives bestowing
   Haunting symphonies may play!

7. *People of all climes and cultures*
   Seek your rapture, heed your call;
   Your mystery transcends earth's spires,
   Its fragrant scent transfiguring all.
   Inner gift, outward enabler,
   Aesthetic seer, prophet humane,
   Inspire our hearts o'er worlds to soar
   Extending far your sweet refrain!

8. *Beauty – you of truth the sister –*
   With ecstasy we do adore.
   Kindling fire, evil's resister,
   Help us to trust you more and more
   That, grasping hands, across all bounds
   Of wealth and colour, sex and creed,
   We globally may hear your wounds
   Whispering, 'Come now, I meet your need!'

I pray, Lord, that the springs of beauty, truth and goodness which are present in me and all your children may produce in me and others a vision of what your world should be like.

Forgive me for viewing our new world with its nuclear threat, ecological problems, and human dilemmas through old spectacles. Help me to be transformed through the Lord's Prayer by the renewing of my mind, that I may see the world in the light of your kingdom.

Week 2

I pray for those in need: for those affected by drought, for those living in city squatter camps, for refugees, for injustice, for those whose minds cannot cope with the burdens thrust upon them.

I pray for relief agencies, for welfare workers, and for all humane prophets of a new age. I pray, yet it is no longer I – we all pray together; I pray, yet it is no longer I – you pray within me.

> O God, you have let me pass the night in peace, let me pass the day in peace. Wherever I may go upon my way which you made peaceable for me, O God, lead my steps.
>> When I have spoken, keep lies away from me.
>> When I am hungry, keep me from murmuring.
>> When I am satisfied, keep me from pride.
>> Calling upon you, I pass the day, O Lord, who has no Lord.

~ Boran, Kenya[21] ~

CONTEMPLATION

Be imitators of God ... and live a life of love.

~ Ephesians 5:1–2 ~

NOTES

1. Adapted from a prayer by N. T. Niles included in *The Unity Book of Prayers*, foreword by D. Paton (London: Geoffrey Chapman, 1969), p. 18.
2. Phineas Fletcher, 'The Divine Lover', in D. H. S. Nicholson and A. H. E. Lee (eds.), *The Oxford Book of English Mystical Verse* (Oxford: Clarendon, 1921), p. 19.
3. Charles de Foucauld – see *Unity Book of Prayers* (op. cit.), p. 43.
4. A prayer offered by a prisoner at Wormwood Scrubs Prison, December 1983, and passed on to the chaplain of the day.
5. Edward Dowden, 'Communion' – see *The Oxford Book of English Mystical Verse* (op. cit.), p. 340.
6. J. Armitage Robinson (ed.), *The Apology of Aristides* (Cambridge University Press, 1983), p. 49.
7. Robert Muller, *New Genesis* (New York: Doubleday, 1984), pp. 191–2.
8. Adapted from the Koran, I.
9. Julian of Norwich, 'Showings' – in the volume on Julian of Norwich in the *Classics of Western Spirituality* (op. cit.), p. 183.
10. Charles Wesley – see *Hymns and Psalms* (op. cit.), Hymn 434, vv. 1, 3, 6, 7.
11. Adapted from *Brihadaranyaka Upanishad* 1, 3, 28.
12. Samuel Greg (1804–76) – see *Hymns and Psalms* (op. cit.), Hymn 158.
13. T. S. Eliot, 'Murder in the Cathedral' (London: Faber & Faber, 1968), p. 94.
14. 'Book of Hours' (1514) – see *Hymns and Psalms* (op. cit.), Hymn 696.
15. St Francis of Assisi, 'Canticle of Brother Sun' – in volume on Francis and Clare in the *Classics of Western Spirituality* by R. J. Armstrong and I. C. Brady (eds), (New York: Paulist Press, 1982), pp. 38–9.

16. Chief Seattle's Testimony – quoted in *Beshara* 9 (1990), pp. 16–17.
17. Ian M. Fraser (1917–) – see *Hymns and Psalms* (op. cit.), Hymn 347.
18. Heinrich Suso (*circa* 1300–66) – see Greene and Gollancz (op. cit.), p. 239.
19. Charles Wesley – quoted in volume on John and Charles Wesley by Frank Whaling (ed.), *Classics of Western Spirituality* (op. cit.), pp. 195–6.
20. John Charles Earle, 'Found of Them that Sought Him Not' – see *The Oxford Book of Mystical Verse* (op. cit.), p. 509.
21. Adapted from a 'Boran' (a prayer), Kenya.

Week 2

Week 3

Monday

APPROACH

For God did not give us a spirit of timidity, but a spirit of power, of love and of self-discipline.

~ 2 Timothy 1:7 ~

PRAISE

How lovely is your dwelling-place,
     O Lord Almighty!
My soul yearns, even faints,
     for the courts of the Lord;
My heart and flesh cry out
     for the living God.
Even the sparrow has found a home,
     and the swallow a nest for herself,
     where she may have her young –
A place near your altar,
     O Lord Almighty, my King and my God.
Blessed are those who dwell in your house;
     they are ever praising you.
Blessed are those whose strength is in you,
     who have set their hearts on pilgrimage.
Better is one day in your courts
     than a thousand elsewhere;
I would rather be a doorkeeper in the house of my God
     than dwell in the tents of the wicked.
For the Lord God is a sun and shield;
     the Lord bestows favour and honour;
No good thing does he withhold
     from those whose walk is blameless.
O Lord Almighty
     blessed is the man who trusts in you.

~ Psalm 84:1–5, 10–12 ~

Week 3

THANKS

It is a beauteous evening, calm and free,
The holy time is quiet as a Nun
Breathless with adoration; the broad sun
Is sinking down in its tranquillity;
The gentleness of heaven broods o'er the Sea:
Listen! The mighty Being is awake,
And doth with his eternal motion make
A sound like thunder – everlastingly.
Dear child! Dear Girl! That walkest with me here,
If thou appear untouched by solemn thought,
Thy nature is not therefore less divine:
Thou liest in Abraham's bosom all the year;
And worshipp'st at the Temple's inner shrine,
God being with thee when we know it not.

~ William Wordsworth[1] ~

I thank you, Lord, for your coming to me through nature, through people, through prayer, through the still small whisper of conscience, and in various other ways. Sometimes your coming is routine, at other times it is more dramatic. Whatever may be the means and the occasion, I thank you for your coming.

I thank you for the innocence of children. They cut through seriousness and blissfully accept the most intense experiences because to them those experiences are natural. Grant me the innocence of a child. May I not be surprised at your coming, but always be ready to awaken to it, and to mark rather when it is not there.

Thank you, Lord, for your arising in me, which seems like a coming, but is my becoming aware of your presence which has always been offered.

SELF-EXAMINATION AND FORGIVENESS

I fled Him, down the nights and down the days;
I fled Him, down the arches of the years;
I fled Him, down the labyrinthine ways
Of my own mind; and in the mist of tears
I hid from Him, and under running laughter,
Up vistaed hopes I sped;
And shot, precipitated,
Adown Titanic glooms of chasmed fears,
From those strong Feet that followed, followed after.
But with unhurrying chase,
And unperturbed pace,
Deliberate speed, majestic instancy,
They beat – and a Voice beat
More instant than the Feet –
'All things betray thee, who betrayest Me.'

~ Francis Thompson[2] ~

Week 3

Forgive me, Lord, for assuming that I had to open up contact with you. Forgive me for my presumption that I was the initiator, that I was in control, that it was all my doing.

All the time you were pursuing and I was reacting to your pursuit. You were seeking, and I was responding to your search.

Now that I recognise your footsteps that went before as well as followed after, I commit myself to you. Help me to hear and see your inner workings within the pathways of my heart, as I accept your forgiveness now, O Lord.

MEDITATION

So I say to you: Ask and it will be given to you; seek and you will find; knock and the door will be open to you. For everyone who asks receives; he who seeks finds; and to him who knocks, the door will be opened.

~ Luke 11:9–10 ~

Sometimes God knocks at the door of our life. Sometimes we knock at his door. Sometimes we hear him say, 'Here I am! I stand at the door and knock. If anyone hears my voice and opens the door, I will come in and eat with him, and he with me.' At other times, as in this passage, it is the other way round. In either case, a voice speaks, and a door opens. The difference lies in this: whose voice is it?

The possibility is that we have opened the door of our life to God in answer to his voice. Perhaps we find it harder to open our mouth, to raise our voice, to ask, to knock on the door of God's love.

Why is this? Is it lack of faith? Is it a belief that we live in a closed world of scientific law that is rigidly determined? Is it a sense that God knows what we want anyway, therefore why ask him? Is it a feeling that if our prayers really were answered it might make life uncomfortable? Is it spiritual shyness, a timidity to trespass upon God's love? There are many possible reasons.

The witness of this passage is clear. Indeed, the New Testament makes astounding claims about praying for others and the effect it can have. As one passage puts it, 'If you believe, you will receive whatever you ask for in prayer.' As another passage puts it, 'the Father will give you whatever you ask in my name'. 'In my name' – in love; 'whatever you ask; – first ask; 'if you believe' – if you trust in God: these are the three qualifications – if we trust in God and ask in love.

In our mind's eye, we see people and situations we wish to pray for. We offer them to God. We put our own love into the person concerned or the situation concerned. We ask God's blessing. We see God's love operating. We see him at work. We ask, we seek, we knock. We see God in the person or situation we are praying for. We see God present and engaged in his transforming work. We see the door beginning to open.

Week 3

We – I – pray now for a particular person especially on our mind. We hold them up; we love them; we ask God's blessing; we see God's love operating; we see him at work; we ask, we seek, we knock; we see God in the person we are praying for; we see God present and engaged in his transforming work; we see the door beginning to open.

PETITION

O God, give me the vision to know who and what to pray for, give me the trust in you to pray with full confidence that fruits may result, and help me to live and pray in love.

1. *O God, what offering shall I give*
        To thee, the Lord of earth and skies?
    My spirit, soul, and flesh receive,
        A holy, living sacrifice:
    Small as it is, 'tis all my store;
    More shouldst thou have, if I had more.

2. *Now, O my God, thou hast my soul,*
        No longer mine, but thine I am;
    Guard thou thine own, possess it whole,
        Cheer it with hope, with love inflame;
    Thou hast my spirit, there display
    Thy glory to the perfect day.

3. *Thou hast my flesh, thy hallowed shrine,*
        Devoted solely to thy will;
    Here let thy light for ever shine,
        This house still let thy presence fill;
    O source of life, live, dwell, and move
    In me, till all my life be love!

4. *Send down thy likeness from above,*
        And let this my adorning be;
    Clothe me with wisdom, patience, love,
        With lowliness and purity,
    Than gold and pearls more precious far,
    And brighter than the morning star.

5. *Lord, arm me with thy Spirit's might,*
        Since I am called by thy great name;
    In thee let all my thoughts unite,
        Of all my works be thou the aim:

Week 3

Thy love attend me all my days,
And my sole business by thy praise.

~ Joachim Lange[3] ~

PRAYERS FOR ACTION

So stood of old the holy Christ
Amidst the suffering throng;
With whom His lightest touch sufficed
To make the weakest strong.

That healing gift He lends to them
Who use it in His name;
The power that filled His garment's hem
Is evermore the same.

For lo! In human hearts unseen
The Healer dwelleth still,
And they who make His temples clean
The best subserve His will.

The holiest task by Heaven decreed,
An errand all divine,
The burden of our common need
To render less is thine.

The paths of pain are thine. Go forth
With patience, trust, and hope;
The sufferings of a sin-sick earth
Shall give thee ample scope.

Beside the unveiled mysteries
Of life and death go stand,
With guarded lips and reverend eyes
And pure of heart and hand.

So shalt thou be with power endued
From Him who went about
The Syrian hillsides doing good,
And casting demons out.

That Good Physician liveth yet
Thy friend and guide to be;
The Healer by Gennesaret
Shall walk the rounds with thee.

~ John Greenleaf Whittier[4] ~

Week 3

CONTEMPLATION

Prayer itself is the essence of the Godhead.

Tuesday

APPROACH

Everyone who asks receives; he who seeks finds; to him who knocks the door will be opened.

~ Matthew 7:8 ~

PRAISE

O God! If I worship Thee in fear of Hell, burn me in Hell; if I worship Thee in hope of Paradise, exclude me from Paradise; but if I worship Thee for Thine own sake, withhold not Thine Everlasting Beauty!

~ Rabi'a[5] ~

O God, I praise you for your everlasting beauty
and for your eternal being.
You are an ocean of love.
You are a fountain of bliss.
You are a light to the world.
You are the joyness of joy.
You are the most good, the most beautiful, the most true.
You are power and glory.
You are perfect holiness.
You are that which you are.
You have eternal communion with the Son and the Spirit.
You offer that communion to me.
Praised by you, incomparable Lord!

THANKS

I thank you, Lord, for the effect of your life on my life.
I thank you for the awareness I have of your reality and being.
I thank you for insight into the meaning of my life.
I thank you for the witness of my five senses to the beauty of your creation.
I thank you for any foothold I may have upon eternal life.
I thank you for my imagination of a fairer future for humankind.
I thank you for my intention to love others.
I thank you for my ability to give thanks.
I thank you because I know that I am a steward of my life.

To your name, O Lord, be thanks and praise.

Week 3

SELF-EXAMINATION AND FORGIVENESS

I have recklessly thrown aside my paternal glory, and among the sinners I have dissipated the wealth which thou gavest me; wherefore I cry to thee with the voice of the Prodigal: I have sinned before thee, O Merciful Father, receive me as a penitent, and make me as one of thy hired servants.

~ Eastern Church Confession ~

Love bade me welcome, yet my soul drew back,
    Guilty of dust and sin.
But quick-ey'd Love, observing me grow slack
    From my first entrance in,
Drew nearer to me, sweetly questioning
    If I lack'd any thing.

'A guest,' I answer'd, 'worthy to be here.'
    Love said, 'You shall be he.'
'I the unkind, ungrateful? Ah my dear,
    I cannot look on thee.'
Love took my hand, and smiling did reply,
    'Who made the eyes but I?'

'Truth Lord, but I have marr'd them; let my shame
    Go where it doth deserve.'
'And know you not,' says Love, 'who bore the blame?'
    'My dear, then I will serve.'
'You must sit down,' says Love, 'and taste my meat.'
    So I did sit and eat.

~ George Herbert[6] ~

MEDITATION

Who shall separate us from the love of Christ? Shall trouble or hardship or persecution or famine or nakedness or danger or sword? As it is written: 'For your sake we face death all day long; we are considered as sheep to be slaughtered.' No, in all these things we are more than conquerors through him who loved us. For I am convinced that neither death nor life, neither angels nor demons, neither the present nor the future, nor any powers, neither height nor depth, nor anything else in all creation, will be able to separate us from the love of God that is in Christ Jesus our Lord.

~ Romans 8:35–9 ~

We are suffering or we know some one who is suffering. Our suffering, like that of Job, may be of three kinds: material suffering – the loss of some of our possessions; physical suffering – some bodily affliction; or mental suffering – nothing makes sense any more.

Week 3

We can try to find an answer to the problem of suffering. God is a God of law, we suggest. He does not overturn laws so that we can avoid suffering. That would mean that we lived in a world of chaos rather than law.

God is a God of free will we suggest. There is little doubt that much suffering is caused by inhumanity. Humans may prefer wrong to right, hatred to love, evil to good. God cannot force them against their will and suffering may occur.

God is a God of community, we suggest. If our own suffering alone were the whole story it would be easier to cope with; but we live in families, communities, towns, states, a world to which we are bound by bonds of relationship. This enlarges the problem of suffering.

God is a God of constructive change, we suggest. If the world were static and unchanging there might be less suffering but then where would be adventure, creative process, onward vision and future goals?

These four reasons alleviate the problem of suffering to some extent. If we had been God would we have made a world without law, without free will, without community, and without constructive change, and therefore without, or with much less, suffering? Probably not! Yet the problem is not solved, it is merely put into a framework of understanding.

Marx said the point is not to understand the world but to change the world. Christ urges us both to understand the world and to change it. Yet in the case of suffering it is perhaps more important to change it than merely to understand it.

'Nothing can separate us from the love of Christ.' God may not directly will our suffering but he does allow it. In allowing it, he gives us the power to transform it. In itself it is often not good. Like Job we are tempted to inveigh against it. But by the mental attitude we bring to it, it can be transformed from a curse to a blessing, from a wound to a salve, from a bane to a boom. A half-full glass of water can be much less than we expect, or much more than we expect, according to how we view it.

More important is to see our suffering in the light of Christ himself. If he transformed two pieces of wood and some nails into the instruments of our redemption, we can, in him, transform our suffering into an instrument of redemption for ourselves and for others. Indeed more than merely changing our suffering into a thing of creative intent by the mental attitude we bring to it, it may well be that in Christ our suffering like his can become vicarious – it can help others directly.

We look at him now. He says, 'Your suffering cannot separate me from you. Let us look at it together and ask what it can do. What can it teach you about yourself? About me? About other people? How can it be used: to bless yourself? To bless me? To bless other people? What part have you to play in the fellowship of my sufferings?' We don't know the answer yet, but we gaze into his face long and hard.

Week 3

PETITION

O God, you have prepared in peace the path I must follow today. Help me to walk straight on that path. If I speak, remove lies from my lips. If I am hungry, take away from me all complaint. If I have plenty, destroy pride in me. May I go through the day calling on you, you O Lord, who know no other Lord.

~ Galla, Ethiopia: a Prayer[7] ~

1. *O Lord and Master of us all,*
     Whate'er our name or sign,
   We own thy sway, we hear thy call,
     We test our lives by thine.

2. *Our thoughts lie open to thy sight;*
     And, maked to thy glance,
   Our secret sins are in the light
     Of thy pure countenance.

3. *Yet, weak and blinded though we be,*
     Thou dost our service own;
   We bring our varying gifts to thee,
     And thou rejectest none.

4. *To thee our full humanity,*
     Its joys and pains belong;
   The wrong of each to each on thee
     Inflicts a deeper wrong.

5. *Who hates, hates thee; who loves, becomes*
     Therein to thee allied;
   All sweet accords of hearts and homes
     In thee are multiplied.

6. *Apart from thee all gain is loss,*
     All labour vainly done;
   The solemn shadow of thy cross
     Is better than the sun.

7. *Our friend, our brother, and our Lord,*
     What may thy service be?
   Nor name, nor form, nor ritual word,
     But simply following thee.

8. *We faintly hear, we dimly see,*
     In differing phrase we pray;

Week 3

But, dim or clear, we own in thee
The Light the Truth, the Way.

~ John Greenleaf Whittier[8] ~

PRAYER FOR ACTION

O God, animate us to cheerfulness. May we have a joyful sense of our blessings, learn to look on the bright circumstances of our lot, and maintain a perpetual contentedness under Thy allotments. Fortify our minds against disappointments and calamity. Preserve us from despondency, from yielding to dejection. Teach us that no evil is intolerable but a guilty conscience; and that nothing can hurt us, if, with true loyalty of affection, we keep Thy commandments, and take refuge in Thee.

~ William Ellery Channing[9] ~

Lord, we pray for those who suffer. We think especially of those who live in hardship every day. We pray for those who live in slums where there are no drains and no proper buildings. We pray for those who have no houses at all, for the outcast, the maimed, the diseased and the tortured in mind. We pray for the hungry, the forsaken, the dying, the lonely. What are our sufferings compared with theirs, Lord?

But you know their sufferings, and we can know them, too, in you. Ignite our imaginations, Lord. And help us to remember that they pray for us at the same time as we pray for them. Use our sufferings that we may be of greater use to your suffering children everywhere.

CONTEMPLATION

The Lord your God will be with you wherever you go.

~ Joshua 1:9 ~

Week 3

Wednesday

Let us love one another, for love comes from God.

PRAISE

How can we picture you, O God,
For whom the very universe
A body doth provide that yet
Cannot begin to countenance who
You are?

But visualise you, Lord, we must –
Immensity does not evoke
Our love or concentrate our thought!
Imagination poor is all
We have.

A beam of light irradiates
The firmament. We see you there.
Yet darkness cannot ban you from
Its portals since you permission
Gave for it to be.

A point of light gives fixity
Of space whereon our mind can dwell
To symbolise your presence. True
Witness this! Yet one that hides as
Well as illuminates the whole.

For though in all the brilliance of
The sums that are or shall be is
Contained a filter of the form
Whereby you lift the veil that
Shrouds your glory –
Surpass it still you do! To those
Of women born 'tis shown in pain

Week 3

That joy begets, in love that hope
Bestows. Humane refractors they
Of brightness pure that angels laud.

Creator, where shall I find you?
High and hidden is your place.
And where shall I not find you?
The world is full of your glory.
I have sought your nearness,
With all my heart I called you
And going out to meet you
I found you coming to meet me.

~ Judah Halevi [10] ~

THANKS

I thank you, Lord, for the glorious gift of life.

I thank you for a body to wash and exercise and respect and use.

I thank you for imagination wherewith to travel to the uttermost parts of my mind.

I thank you for the literature of the ages that feeds and stimulates my mind.

I thank you for my fellows: for my family, my friends, my workmates, my colleagues of every sort.

I thank you for good food to eat, pure water to drink, a nice house in which to live, a safe environment in which to prosper, and the health with which to enjoy these gifts.

I thank you, Lord, that I can go deep into my heart, that I can raise my voice on high, and say thank you for all the gifts of your love!

SELF-EXAMINATION AND FORGIVENESS

Could my heart but see Creation as God sees it – from within;
See His grace behind its beauty, see His will behind its force;
See the flame of life shoot upward when the April days begin;
See the wave of life rush upward from its pure eternal source;

Could I see the summer sunrise glow with God's transcendent hope;
See His peace upon the waters in the moonlit summer night;
See Him nearer still when, blinded, in the depths of gloom I grope, –
See the darkness flash and quiver with the gladness of His light;

Week 3

Could I see the red-hot passion of His love resistless burn
  Through the dumb despair of winter, through the frozen lifeless clod; –
Could I see what lies around me as God sees it, I should learn
  That its outward life is nothing, that its inward life is God.

Vain the dream! To spirit only is the spirit-life revealed;
  God alone can see God's glory: God alone can feel God's love.
By myself the soul of Nature from myself is still concealed;
  And the earth is still around me, and the skies are still above.

Vain the dream! I cannot mingle with the all-sustaining soul;
  I am prisoned in my senses; I am pinioned by my pride;
I am severed by my selfhood from the world-life of the Whole;
  And my world is near and narrow, and God's world is vast and wide.

Vain the dream! Yet in the morning, when the eastern skies are red,
  When the dew is in the meadows, when the lark soars up and sings, –
Leaps a sudden flame within me from its ashes pale and dead,
  And I see God's beauty burning through the veil of outward things.

Brighter grows the veil and clearer, till, beyond all fear and doubt,
  I am ravished by God's splendour into oneness with His rest;
And I draw the world within me, and I send my soul without;
  And God's pulse is in my bosom, and I lie upon God's breast.

Dies the beatific vision in the moment of its birth;
  Dies, but in its death transfigures all the sequence of my days;
Dies, but dying crowns with triumph all the travail of the earth,
  Till its harsh discordant murmurs swell into a psalm of praise.

Then a yearning comes upon me to be drawn at last by death,
  Drawn into the mystic circle in which all things live and move,
Drawn into the mystic circle of the love which is God's breath, –
  Love creative, love receptive, love of loving, love of love.

God! The One, the All of Being! Let me lose my life in Thine;
  Let me be what Thou hast made me, be a quiver of Thy flame.
Purge myself from self's pollution; burn it into life divine;
  Burn it till it dies triumphant in the firespring whence it came.

~ Edmond Gore Alexander Holmes[11] ~

MEDITATION

So he got up from the meal, took off his outer clothing, and wrapped a towel round his waist. After that, he poured water into a basin and began to wash his disciples' feet, drying them with the towel that was wrapped round him.

Week 3

He came to Simon Peter, who said to him, 'Lord, are you going to wash my feet?' Jesus replied, 'You do not realise now what I am doing, but later you will understand'.

'No,' said Peter, 'you shall never wash my feet.' Jesus answered, 'Unless I wash you, you have no part with me.'

'Then, Lord,' Simon Peter replied, 'not just my feet but my hands and my head as well!'

~ John 13:4–9 ~

This passage speaks to us at four levels. We go through them in mediation one by one.

In the east, the disciple salutes the master or guru by touching the feet of the beloved preceptor. Rarely, if at all, does it happen the other way round. In India to this day, some privileged families are attended constantly by servants who supply them even with a glass of water. It is no surprise that Peter protests when Jesus prepares to wash his feet. It is a dramatic gesture. Above all else, says Jesus, if someone wants to follow me, they must be ready to serve. They must be ready to be the servants of all. We pause as Jesus comes and washes our feet.

Jesus's washing the disciples' feet is also a symbolic gesture of love as when the expensive ointment is poured over his feet. Jesus can say the words with his mouth, now he demonstrates them with his hands. He is still washing our feet. As he does so, we hear him say 'I love you.' He gazes into our eyes as he speaks.

At a deeper level, the dust on our feet represents the dust that accumulates on our soul. It represents our sins. As Jesus gazes into our eyes while he is washing our feet, we hear him say, 'I love you and I forgive you.' We protest that we don't need to be forgiven. Jesus is adamant. As he washes our feet, and loves us, and forgives us, we say with Peter, 'Alright, we understand now, forgive us to the depths, wash our hands and head as well.'

One final point. This is a daily happening. Each day, Jesus washes our feet in service; each day he says, 'I love you'; each day we accumulate dust on the texture of our soul that distances us from him and makes it less easy for us effectively to serve others. Each day he washed that dust away from us through forgiveness.

'Thank you, Lord, but not forgiveness again,' we say. He replies, 'Not once, but seventy times seven.' He stoops and washes our feet.

PETITION

O God, who hast taught us that all our doings without love are nothing worth, send down thy Holy Spirit and pour into our hearts that most excellent gift of love, the very bond of peace and of all virtues, without which whosoever liveth is counted dead before thee.

Week 3

PRAYERS FOR ACTION

O God our Father, I pray for those known to me, and for all those in our world who are suffering from injustice. I pray:

For those who are discriminated against because of their race, colour or religion.

For those imprisoned for working for the relief of oppression.

For those who are hounded for speaking the inconvenient truth.

For those tempted to violence as a cry against overwhelming hardship.

For those deprived of reasonable health and education.

For those suffering from hunger and famine.

For those too weak to help themselves and who have no one to help them.

For the unemployed, who cry out for work but do not find it.

I pray for anyone of my own acquaintance who is personally affected by injustice.

Forgive me, Lord, if I unwittingly share in the conditions or in a system that perpetuates injustice.

Show me how I can serve your children and make your love practical by washing their feet.

Pray for me that I loose not my grip on the hands of Jesus even under the guise of ministering to the poor.

~ Mother Teresa of Calcutta ~

CONTEMPLATION

A Christian is a lord of all, subject to none.
A Christian is a servant of all, subject to all.

~ Adapted from Martin Luther ~

Week 3

Thursday

To him who is thirsty I will give to drink without cost from the spring of the water of life.

~ Revelation 21:6 ~

PRAISE

We praise you, O God, for your gift of love.

Because we are who we are, we find it difficult really to believe that you are Love. We recoil from it because it seems to be too good to be true or because our human experience holds us back.

Yet we know that you are Love, and we praise you for it.

Flood us with your love we pray, O God, that in knowing it we may give it, and in giving it we may know it more,

We praise you for the glimpses we have had of your love.

We praise you because we know that you are an ocean of love in which we can bathe.

We praise you because although your love is shed abroad in the world, it is also directed at us.

We praise you because you love us as we are now. For us, for us, your love streams forth. We praise you, O God who art Love.

THANKS

1. *'Lord, I must see the world in all*
   Its splendour' was my cry. He said,
   'Go forth and see the trees stand tall,
   And listen to the birds the north
   Wind serenade, then come and tell
   How nature worked with you her spell!'

2. *Earth, sea and sky I scanned as night*
   Shook hands with day. The cycle once again
   Its drama played as looked I right

Week 3

Into the stars above, the dewy rain,
And everything below, to find
An earth full beautiful and kind.

3. *Confused I went unto the Lord.*
   He smiled and answered not a word.
   My gaze fell inward full intent
   To banish flower and bee and scent
   For my purview. No more should time
   Be spent unravelling their rhyme!

4. *Tingled my inner ear with fragrance*
   Far beyond the power of thought to grasp.
   Within a garden rose, a lance
   Of beauty, causing me to gasp
   In ecstasy! My soul within
   Me grew, the world encompassing.

5. *The summons came again 'Begone!'*
   Methought the brook became a flow
   Of energy divine, the grass a throng
   Of angel choirs, the flower's show
   A flame supernal taken now
   From soul within to bush and bough!

~ F.W. ~

Thanks be to you, Lord, for all your gifts.
I thank you for the gift of nature with its colours, scents and sounds.
I thank you for the gift of people in all their complexity.
I thank you for the gift of yourself and your grace.
I thank you too for the ladder that joins these gifts together helping me to understand each by means of the other.
Give me insight into all your gifts, and you the Giver.
Thus may thanks lead to thanks and to more thanks and to contentment.

SELF-EXAMINATION AND FORGIVENESS

Psalm 103

1. *Praise the Lord, O my soul;*
   all my inmost being, praise his holy name.
2. *Praise the Lord, O my soul,*
   and forget not all his benefits –
3. *who forgives all your sins*
   and heals all your diseases,

Week 3

4. *who redeems your life from the pit*
   and crowns you with love and compassion,
5. *who satisfies your desires with good things*
   so that your youth is renewed like the eagle's.
6. *The Lord works righteousness*
   and justice for all the oppressed.
7. *He made known his ways to Moses,*
   his deeds to the people of Israel:
8. *The Lord is compassionate and gracious,*
   slow to anger, abounding in love.
9. *He will not always accuse,*
   nor will he harbour his anger for ever;
10. *he does not treat us as our sins deserve*
    or repay us according to our iniquities.
11. *For as high as the heavens are above the earth,*
    so great is his love for those who fear him;
12. *as far as the east is from the west,*
    so far has he removed our transgressions from us.

MEDITATION

John was an old tailor of York. He was innocent and without guile. His wife was dead, his children gone, and he was alone.

One day he read about the beatific vision. He had not heard much about that in the little chapel he attended. If it is about seeing God face to face I want to do that before I die, he said to himself, but I don't know how to go about it.

He went into his shop the next day. He could have retired but he liked to keep it open to sell, to talk, and to help. A smart man came in. He was due to be made mayor that day. 'Here is your robe,' said John. 'Thank you,' he said, 'and here is your money. But before I go I want to tell you something that has been on my mind. I asked you to make the robe so that I could talk with you. When I was younger, I set out on my journey to be mayor by an act of cheating, and I am having qualms about going ahead with the ceremony.' John listened and said, 'What is past is past. Go ahead to lead our town with honesty. That is the best way to make amends.' After a short prayer, the mayor went away smiling.

A woman and two young children circled around John's shop. The children were nicely dressed, the woman was not. 'Come in,' said John, 'what can I do for you?' 'I am on social security,' said the woman, 'and although I can clothe my children, I have not enough to clothe myself well. But I have to go to a wedding of a great friend.' 'Choose yourself a dress,' said John, 'and take it with my love.' The woman and children went away smiling.

Week 3

A shabbily dressed young man came in. 'Here it is,' said John, handing him a parcel. 'I think you will find it fits well – and good luck with your interview.' The young man lingered, and eventually tried on the suit. His appearance was transformed. 'Don't worry about the money,' said John, 'you can pay me later if all goes well.' He went away smiling.

In came a middle-aged man John didn't know. He looked like a miner and, sure enough, he explained that he had been made redundant and was moving to another town. 'I have something I want to confess,' he said. 'When we were on strike I had no money to feed the family, and one day I stole this from you.' He produced a parcel in which there was a smart suit and gave it to John. John took it, and opened the envelope given to him by the mayor in which there was twice the amount he had been owed. He gave half of it to the visitor. He said, 'You need a suit as well, take this other one!' The visitor could hardly believe it, and he protested, but in the end he went away smiling.

John looked in the suit he had been handed. Stuck in one of the pockets was part of an evening newspaper, and a piece of paper on which was some writing. He looked at the piece of paper, then he looked at the newspaper. It contained a photo of the mayor and a copy of his opening speech, a photo of a smartly dressed woman with two children on her way to a wedding, and a photo of a young man who had been out of work for three years shaking hands with his new employer. John smiled, but as he gazed at the photographs smiling back at him, they took on a radiant dazzle, flew out of the page at him, and seemed to become like angels escorting him he knew not where.

The doctor said, 'He must have gone instantly. There was a beautiful glow on his face, and he was holding a piece of paper which read "Blessed are the pure in heart, for they will see God."'

PETITION

1. *Being of beings, God of love,*
    To thee our hearts we raise:
    Thy all-sustaining power we prove,
    And gladly sing thy praise.

2. *Thine, wholly thine, we long to be:*
    Our sacrifice receive;
    Made, and preserved, and saved by thee,
    To thee ourselves we give.

3. *Heav'nward our every wish aspires;*
    For all thy mercies' store,

Week 3

The sole return thy love requires
Is that we ask for more.

4. *For more we ask; we open then*
   Our hearts to embrace thy will;
   Turn and revive us, Lord, again,
   With all thy fullness fill.

5. *Come, Holy Ghost, the Saviour's love*
   Shed in our hearts abroad;
   So shall we ever live, and move,
   And be with Christ in God.

~ Charles Wesley [12] ~

PRAYER FOR ACTION

Eleven Suggestions for Love in Action

1. Serve those whom you expect to serve you.
2. Consider no person inferior, but recognise limitations.
3. Lead men and women by action and example.
4. Be humble in speaking about your accomplishments.
5. Teach and be taught.
6. Attack unfairness from any quarter.
7. Believe that your employees must prosper if you are to prosper.
8. Seek the truth no matter who may get hurt.
9. Pray for God's guidance when you must make a decision affecting the life and future of any person.
10. Make your own decision based on your own best judgement only after careful consideration has been given to ALL the facts.
11. Forgive honest mistakes where the person making the mistake is honestly self-critical. If people are not self-critical, they must learn to be or they can never successfully supervise others or develop to their best abilities.

~ Morton Kelsey [13] ~

CONTEMPLATION

If we love one another, God lives in us and his love is made complete in us.

~ 1 John 4:12 ~

Week 3

Friday

APPROACH

Set your hearts on things above.

~ Colossians 3:1 ~

PRAISE

God is our refuge and strength,
an ever-present help in trouble.
Therefore we will not fear, though the earth give way
and the mountains fall into the heart of the sea.
Though its waters roar and foam and the mountains quake
with their surging.
There is a river whose streams make glad the city of God,
the holy place where the Most High dwells.
God is within her, she will not fall;
God will help you at break of day.
Nations are in uproar, kingdoms fall;
he lifts his voice, the earth melts.
The Lord God Almighty is with us,
the God of Jacob is our fortress.
Be still and know that I am God;
I will be exalted among the nations,
I will be exalted in the earth.

~ Psalm 46:1–7, 10 ~

THANKS

1. *My God, I thank thee, who has made*
       The earth so bright,
   So full of splendour and of joy,
       Beauty and light;
   So many glorious things are here,
       Noble and right.

2. *I thank thee, Lord, that thou hast made*
       Joy to abound,

So many gentle thoughts and deeds
    Circling us round,
That in the darkest spot of earth
    Some love is found.

3. I thank thee too that often joy
    Is touched with pain,
That shadows fall on brightest hours,
    That thorns remain,
So that Earth's bliss may be our guide,
    And not our chain.

4. I thank thee, Lord, that thou hast kept
    The best in store;
We have enough, yet not too much
    To long for more –
A yearning for a deeper peace
    Not known before.

5. I thank thee, Lord, that here our lives,
    Though amply blest,
Can never find, although they seek,
    a perfect rest,
Nor ever shall, until we lean
    On Jesu's breast.

~ Adelaide Anne Proctor[14] ~

SELF-EXAMINATION AND FORGIVENESS

Lord, come away!
    Why dost Thou stay?
Thy road is ready; and Thy paths made straight
    With longing expectations wait
The consecration of Thy beauteous feet.
    Ride on triumphantly; behold, we lay
    Our lusts and proud wills in Thy way!

Hosanna! Welcome to our hearts! Lord, here
Thou hast a temple too; as full and dear
    As that of Sion, and as full of sin:
Nothing but thieves and robbers dwell therein:
Enter, and chase them forth, and cleanse the floor:
    Crucify them, that they may never more
    Profane that holy place

Where Thou hast chose to set Thy face!
And then if our still tongues shall be
Mute in the praises of Thy deity,
The stones out of the temple wall
Shall cry aloud and call
Hosanna! And Thy glorious footsteps greet!

~ Jeremy Taylor[15] ~

Lord, I can only examine as much of myself as I know. Forgive the shortcomings of which I am aware as I name them now slowly in your sight.

Grant, O Lord, that in becoming more sensitive to the reality of who I am, I may become more aware of the depths of your nature.

So will my need for forgiveness increase as I know myself more in your light.

In receiving your greater forgiveness, I will thank you the more.

MEDITATION

Many names have been given to Jesus. We look at some of the names given to Jesus in St John's Gospel. We do not comment on them. We look at them – and we look at him.

First of all, we enter our own inner room. We are quiet in the silence of our own inner peace as we sit patient and still. When we are in a state of equilibrium, we bring before our mind a name of Jesus, and as we do so we see Jesus coming and sitting opposite us. We do not reflect upon the various nuances of the name. We repeat it aloud to ourselves again and again as we look at him. We use 'You' instead of 'I' in saying the name, otherwise we repeat it aloud. Then we pass on to the next name. We take as long on each name as we feel comfortable with, but ten times should be a minimum with a pause in between. As we finish saying one name, we leave time for that name to go, and we wait for the next name to come before we begin to say it. All the time we look at Jesus.

You are the Lamb of God who takes away the sin
of the world. ~ 1:29 ~

You are the bread of life. ~ 6:35 ~

You are the light of the world. ~ 8:12 ~

You are the good shepherd. ~ 10:14 ~

You are the way, the truth and the life. ~ 14:6 ~

You are the true vine. ~ 15:1 ~

Week 3

Now we leave the time-honoured names behind. We invent our own names for Jesus. What does he mean to us? We picture him in the same form as we repeat one or more times our own names for him.

Finally the names die away. We can think of no more.

Except for one: we say out aloud, 'My Lord and my God!'

We say it again and again.

PETITION

I would have you never cease increasing the fuel for the fire of holy desire, that is, the wood of self-knowledge. This is the wood that nourishes and feeds the fire of divine love; this love is acquired by the knowledge of self and of the inestimable love of God . . . The more fuel one gives to the fire, so much the more increases the warmth of love of Christ and of neighbour. So remain hidden in the knowledge of self.

~ Catherine of Siena[16] ~

Grant, Lord, that in coming closer to you, I may come closer to myself, and in coming closer to myself I may come closer to you. In so doing, may I come closer to other people, and may they come closer to me.

PRAYER FOR ACTION

Decide to be happy
render others happy
proclaim your joy
love passionately your miraculous life
do not listen to promises
do not wait for a better world
be grateful for every moment of life
switch on and keep on the positive buttons in yourself, those marked optimism,
*   serenity, confidence, positive thinking, love*
pray and thank God every day
meditate – smile – laugh
whistle – sing – dance
look with fascination at everything
fill your lungs and heart with liberty
be yourself fully and immensely
*   act like a king or queen unto Death*
*   feel God in your body, mind, heart, and soul*
*   and be convinced of eternal life and resurrection.*

~ Robert Muller[17] ~

1. *Wherever humans share their cares,*
   In bazaar's marts, in jungle lairs,
   There you abide, O Lord!

Week 3

Among the souls by drugs oppressed,
Where throng the crowds by thrills obsessed,
Your mercy is abroad!

2. *No stone is turned outside your ken,*
   No wood is cleaved beyond the pen –
   Dulum of your concern!
   Every event in time engaged,
   The smallest hope of every age,
   Within your mind doth turn!

3. *Human free will, by you allowed,*
   Dispenses joy and pain around
   The drama of life's stage;
   Within your flexible design,
   Your caring love's compelling sign
   Is sketched on every page!

4. *Our place within the total plan*
   Evolving now for every man
   And woman secretly,
   Though partly set by gene and race,
   By disposition, time and place,
   Within your will is free!

5. *So now may we the witness know*
   Within our pilgrimage below
   Of your indwelling love;
   That engaged fully by your care,
   In sacrificial service here,
   Your Spirit we may prove![18]

CONTEMPLATION

For me to live is Christ and to die is gain.

~ Philippians 1:21 ~

Week 3

Saturday

APPROACH

In quietness and trust is your strength.

~ Isaiah 30:15 ~

PRAISE

The heavens declare the glory of God:
the skies proclaim the work of his hands.
Day after day they pour forth speech;
night after night they display knowledge.
There is no speech or language
where their voice is not heard.
Their voice goes out into all the earth,
their words to the ends of the world.
The law of the Lord is perfect,
reviving the soul.
The statutes of the Lord are trustworthy,
making wise the simple.
The precepts of the Lord are right,
giving joy to the heart.
The commands of the Lord are radiant,
giving light to the eyes.
The fear of the Lord is pure,
enduring for ever.
The ordinances of the Lord are sure
and altogether righteous.
They are more precious than gold,
than much pure gold.
May the words of my mouth and the
meditation of my heart
be pleasing in your sight,
O Lord, my Rock and my Redeemer.

~ Psalm 19:1–4, 7–10, 14 ~

Week 3

THANKS

1. *There is a book (who runs may read)*
    Which heavenly truth imparts,
    And all the lore its scholars need,
    Pure eyes and Christian hearts.

2. *The works of God above, below,*
    Within us and around,
    Are pages in that book, to show
    How God himself is found.

3. *The glorious sky, embracing all,*
    Is like the Maker's love,
    Wherewith encompassed, great and small
    In peace and order move.

4. *One name, above all glorious names,*
    With its ten thousand tongues
    The everlasting sea proclaims,
    Echoing angelic songs.

5. *The raging fire, the roaring wind,*
    Thy boundless power display;
    And in the gentler breeze we find
    Thy Spirit's viewless way.

6. *Two worlds are ours: 'tis only sin*
    Forbids us to descry
    The mystic heaven and earth within,
    Plain as the sea and sky.

7. *Thou who has given me eyes to see*
    And love this sight so fair,
    Give me a heart to find out thee,
    And read thee everywhere.

~ John Keble[19] ~

SELF-EXAMINATION AND FORGIVENESS

O Lord, I come before you to confess my sins. Grant that, to the extent that I know my own shortcomings, I may not conceal them from you.

Week 3

I confess the sins to do with my body, the sins to do with my mind, and the sins that belong to my soul.

I confess the sins left over from my youth, and the sins of my maturity.

I confess the sins I know about, and offer to you the sins I do not know about.

I confess the sins that lie open to me and to others, and the secret sins known only to me.

I confess the sins intended to further my own designs, and the sins intended to further the designs of others.

By your mercy may I know your forgiveness, Lord. By the indwelling of your Spirit grant that day by day your grace may grow within me so that the fruits of your Spirit may abide.

MEDITATION

I will not cease from Mental Fight,
Nor shall my Sword sleep in my hand,
Till we have built Jerusalem,
In England's green and pleasant Land.

~ William Blake[20] ~

Then I saw a new heaven and a new earth.

~ Revelation 21:1 ~

For the purposes of our meditation, Blake's words may more appropriately be read: 'Till we have built a new community on the face of the globe.' How can we build 'a new earth'? How can we conceive of God's will being done on earth as it is in heaven? This earth with this morning's newspaper headlines? This earth with its threat of nuclear war? This earth whose deserts are growing, forests decreasing, and ozone layer being threatened? This earth with its poverty, famine, refugees, racial discrimination, lack of human rights? This earth with its search for meaning and its spiritual malaise?

I pause from mental effort. I become silent. I enter the room of my inner spirit to be alone. I realise God's presence.

I visualise the globe in the inner chamber of my mind. I see it spinning round. I see its oceans, islands, continents, mountains, forests and lakes. I see them connected to each other. I hear a whisper, 'This is my world, this is my creation, these are my resources.'

I visualise the globe again I see it spinning round. I see its nations, its people of different colours, its religions, its cultures, its family of human beings. I hear a whisper, 'These are my children, these are my peoples, these are my human resources.'

I see the potentialities of the globe under God's gaze: the riches of different cultures, the stock of human intelligence, the reservoir of human love, the human will to create peace, the creative sense of human awe and wonder, the human energy for justice and global co-operation, the untapped spiritual resources. I see their potential for joy and long-term hope. I see darkness and negativity and pain being overcome. The vision of the globe fades. I am alone with God in my inner room.

I hear the words, 'Be you transformed by the renewing of your mind.' I ask what that means. In a flash I see the globe begin to spin in my mind again: there is adequate food and good drinking water for every human; there is reasonable shelter and health for every human; there are opportunities for education and work for every human; human rights and a safe environment are available to every human; war is no longer feared; and different cultures and religions share their treasures. 'On earth as it is in heaven.'

I say to the Lord, 'I think I see: my inward renewal is part of a wider renewal of the whole human community.' The globe spins again. The words are uttered at each stage of the revolution of the globe, 'Whom shall I send, and who will go for us to take part in the renewal of this world?' With joy I see men and women rising up everywhere. I rise and say, 'Here am I: send me.'

PETITION

Teach us, Lord, that the more we give, the more we have.
Teach us, Lord, that in order to change the world,
we must also change ourselves.

~ Nachman of Bratzlav[21] ~

1. *We turn to you, O God of every nation,*
       Giver of life and origin of good;
   Your love is at the heart of all creation,
       Your hurt is people's broken brotherhood.

2. *We turn to you, that we may be forgiven*
       For crucifying Christ on earth again;
   We know that we have never wholly striven,
       Forgetting self, to love the other man.

3. *Free every heart from pride and self-reliance;*
       Our ways of thought inspire with simple grace;
   Break down among us barriers of defiance;
       Speak to the soul of all the human race.

4. *On men who fight on earth for right relations*
       We pray the light of love from hour to hour,
   Grant wisdom to the leaders of the nations,
       The gift of carefulness to those in power.

5. *Teach us, good Lord, to serve the needs of others;*
   Help us to give and not to count the cost;
   Unite us all, for we are born as brothers;
   Defeat our Babel with your Pentecost.

~ Fred Kaan [22] ~

PRAYERS FOR ACTION

The world cries out with longing hope,
Her heartbeat echoing long,
'With valour faint why should I grope,
Renewal is my song!'

Echoes of war, nature's dismay,
Pollution, famine, fear,
Their ardour sharp seek to display:
Salvation yet is near.

Demons of envy, lust and pride
Stalk human hearts abroad,
Yet can their progeny abide?
O God, new hope afford!

In human bosoms deep, O Lord,
A sense of wonder yearns;
A feel for peace and just accord
Awakens, grows, and burns!

The soaring mount and verdant vale
Respond with throbbing life,
'May peace 'twixt man and earth prevail,
Away with weakening strife!'

The star-clad universe on high
Refracts the voice divine,
'Your teenage-pangs now leave behind,
O world, your life refine!'

Repent, reform, relive, revive.
Your tumult turn to joy,
Exalt with hope, new bliss imbibe!
My form who can destroy?

O human race, chastised, forgiven,
O globe, beloved earth,
For your unveiling saints have striven,
In God find your rebirth!'

Week 3

Ten Global Commands

1. You shall love each other, your planet, your family, the God of the universe and your own miraculous life with all your heart, all your soul, all your mind and all your strength.
2. You shall practise truth, kindness and tolerance towards each other.
3. You shall never kill a human brother or sister, not even in the name of a nation.
4. You shall not produce, trade, wear or use any arms or instruments of violence.
5. You shall never be violent, either physically or verbally, towards each other.
6. You shall respect the lives, peace, happiness and uniqueness of all your human brothers and sisters.
7. You shall co-operate with each other, help each other and inspire each other.
8. You shall contribute your peace, love and happiness to the peace, love and happiness of the human family.
9. You shall live in harmony with yourself, with your parents, with your children, with your environment, with all humanity and with the God of the universe.
10. You shall live a responsible life in accord with the supreme interests of our planet and of the human family.

CONTEMPLATION

Your kingdom come, your will be done on earth as it is in heaven.

~ Matthew 6:10 ~

Sunday

APPROACH

APPROACH

Glory to God in the highest, on earth peace and goodwill towards men.

·- Luke 2:10 ~

PRAISE

1. *Awake, awake to love and work*
       The lark is in the sky,
    The fields are wet with diamond dew,
       The worlds awake to cry
    Their blessings on the Lord of life,
       As he goes meekly by.

2. *Come, let thy voice be one with theirs,*
       Shout with their shout of praise;
    See how the giant sun roars up,
       Great lord of years and days!
    So let the love of Jesus come,
       And set thy soul ablaze –

3. *To give and give and give again*
       What God has given thee,
    To spend thyself nor count the cost,
       To serve right gloriously
    The God who gave all worlds that are,
       And all that are to be.

~ G. A. Studdert-Kennedy[23] ~

THANKS

I thank you, Lord, for the wonderful diversity of the world in which I live. I thank you for the many colours I see with my eyes. I thank you for the different races of humanity.

I thank you for the different parts of my body and the way in which they support one another. I thank you for Jesus, who was born a Jew but is

Week 3

now worshipped in every land. I thank you for the different religious and cultures of our world and the mutual enrichment they offer. I thank you for my unique life, and the unique life of my fellow humans on this planet.

I thank you also for the things that bind us all together:

For the one earth which is our birthright, and on which we must live.

For the oneness of humanity transcending our diversity.

For the one God superintending us all.

For the one body in which Christians are joined together.

Help me to rejoice in the unique life that is mine, and to see it as a gift from my heavenly Father to his child. Help me so to use it that your other children may be nourished, that your earth may be cherished, that your kingdom may be furthered, and that your name may be glorified.

SELF-EXAMINATION AND FORGIVENESS

Oh, tempt me not! I love too well this snare
Of silken cords.
Nay, Love, the flesh is fair;
So tempt me not! This earth affords
Too much delight;
Withdraw Thee from my sight,
Lest my weak soul break free
And throw me back to Thee!

Thy Face is all too marred. Nay, Love, not I –
I did not that! Doubtless Thou hadst to die:
Others did faint for Thee; but I faint not.
Only a little while hath sorrow got
The better of me now; for Thou art grieved,
Thinking I need Thee. Oh, Christ, lest I fall
Weeping between Thy Feet, and give Thee all:
Oh, Christ, lest love condemn me unreprieved
into Thy bondage, be it not believed
That Thou hast need of me!

Dost Thou not know
I never turned aside to mock Thy Woe?
I had respect to Thy great love for men:
Why wilt Thou, then,
Question of each new lust –
'Are those not ashes, and is this not dust?'
Ah, Love, Thou hast not eyes
To see how sweet it is!
Each for himself be wise:
Mock not my bliss!

Week 3

Ere Thou cam'st troubling, was I not content?
    Because I pity Thee, and would be glad
        to go mine own way, and not leave Thee sad,
Is all my comfort spent!

Go Thine own ways, nor dream Thou needest me!
Yet if, again, Thou on the bitter Tree
Were hanging now, with none to succour Thee
    Or run to quench Thy sudden cry of thirst,
        Would I not be the first –
Ah, Love, the prize! –
To lift one cloud of suffering from Thine eyes?

        Oh, Christ, let be!
Stretch not Thine ever-pleading Hands thus wide,
Nor with imperious gesture touch Thy Side!
Past is Thy Calvary. By the Life that died,
        Oh, tempt not me!

Nay, if Thou weepest, then I must weep too,
Sweet Tempter, Christ! Yet what can I undo,
        I, the undone, the undone,
        To comfort Thee, God's Son?
Oh, draw me near, and, for some lowest use,
        That I may be
        Lost and undone in Thee
Me from mine own self loose!

~ Laurence Housman[24] ~

MEDITATION

On the last and greatest day of the Feast, Jesus stood and said in a loud voice, 'If anyone is thirsty, let him come to me and drink. Whoever believes in me, as the Scripture has said, streams of living water will flow from within him.'

~ John 7:37–8 ~

I go into the inner room of my being. Jesus is there. He is saying in a loud voice, 'If anyone is thirsty, let him come to me and drink: streams of living water will flow from within him.' I see him saying these words. I see and hear him saying them over and over again.

After a time, he stops speaking. Now I begin to say the words and as I say them, I think about them. 'If anyone . . . '; can this be true? Anyone? Beggar, prince, harlot? People of every race, sex, age and colour? At any time, in any age, anywhere? '. . . is thirsty'; thirsty for what? For drink? For spiritual refreshment? For both? '. . . let him come'; how? On foot, by transport, within the mind? '. . . to me'; to Christ? Where is Christ?

Confined, free, within, without? '. . . streams of living water'; what kind of water is this? Not flowing water, but living water? Can it be the Holy Spirit? '. . . will flow from within him'; flow where? Flow around, inside, outward to others? How will it flow?

Having churned all the ideas, I become silent again. I fix my inward eyes on Christ, and put on one side the ideas I have explored. They have served their purpose. I repeat the words silently, concentrating on them and on Christ. I engage in the loving silence of repetition.

Is that the Holy Spirit I feel moving within my heart?

PETITION

1. *Jesus, I fain would find*
   Thy zeal for God in me,
   Thy yearning pity for mankind,
   Thy burning charity.

2. *In me thy Spirit dwell;*
   In me thy mercies move:
   So shall the fervour of my zeal
   Be thy pure flame of love.

~ Charles Wesley[25] ~

PRAYER FOR ACTION

Inset into the verdure dim
That is the outward vesture of
A hidden slime untouched by hand
Of human or (it seems) divine
There is a grit of brilliance, gilt
With light, that mocks the darkness dreer –
Its lone abode.

Like a flower that scorns the nuclear blight
It gives, fine jewel that it is!,
A radiance new to what before
Seemed stale, a fragrance sweet to what
Before seemed dank – a symbol sure
Of coming transformation of
The mud in which 'tis cast.

And when we look, O Lord, at all
The troubles of our world they seem
(Malign thought hurled) as shadows set

Week 3

To magnify the truth immured
Within despair. The jewel of
Your kingdom shines to change decay
To dazzling hope.

We pray, Lord, for the gift of your Holy Spirit continually to flow from within us, changing decay to dazzling hope, and magnifying the truth immured within despair.

As we look around, we see many people living lives of quiet despair. Help us to bring to them streams of living water so that the jewels within their lives made be laid bare.

May the jewel of your kingdom shine within the darkest places of earth. For nothing can be hidden from the penetration of your Spirit.

CONTEMPLATION

Every good and perfect gift is from above.

~ James 1:17 ~

NOTES

1. William Wordsworth (1770–1850), 'It is a Beauteous Evening' – see *Batsford Book of Religious Verse* (London: Batsford, 1981), p. 28.
2. Francis Thompson (1859–1907) – see 'The Hound of Heaven', *The Oxford Book of Mystical Verse* (op. cit.), pp. 409–10.
3. Joachim Lange (1670–1744), trans. by John Wesley (1703–91) – see *Hymns and Psalms* (op. cit.), Hymn 801.
4. John Greenleaf Whittier (1807–92), 'The Healer' – see *English Religious Verse* (op. cit.), pp. 192–3.
5. Rabi'a (died 801) – see A. J. Arberry, *Sufism* (London: Allen & Unwin, 1950), pp. 42–3.
6. George Herbert, 'Love' – see volume on George Herbert in *Classics of Western Spirituality*, p. 316 (note 9).
7. 'Galla', Ethiopia, a Prayer – see F. Humphries, *Heart of Prayer* (Nashville: Broadman Press, *circa* 1980), p. 28.
8. John Greenleaf Whittier (1807–92) – see *Hymns and Psalms* (op. cit.), Hymn 717.
9. William Ellery Channing (1780–1842) – see Greene and Gollancz (op. cit.), p. 51.
10. Judah Halevi – see *Heart of Prayer* (op. cit.), p. 68.
11. Edward Gore Alexander Holmes, 'Nirvana' – see *The Oxford Book of English Mystical Verse* (op. cit.), pp. 384–6.
12. Charles Wesley – see *Hymns and Psalms* (op. cit.), Hymn 690.
13. Morton Kelsey, *Caring* (New York: Paulist Press,1981), pp. 151–2.

Week 3

14. Adelaide Anne Proctor (1825–64) – see *Hymns and Psalms* (op. cit.), Hymn 564.
15. Jeremy Taylor (1613–67), 'Hymn for Advent' – see *English Religious Verse* (op. cit.), pp. 95–6.
16. Catherine of Siena – quoted in Morton Kelsey, *Caring* (op. cit.), p. 49.
17. Robert Muller, *New Genesis* (op. cit.), p. 154.
18. Unascribed poems are the author's own.
19. John Keble (1792–1866) – see *Hymns and Psalms* (op. cit.), Hymn 34.
20. William Blake (1757–1827) – *Hymns for Church and School* (London: Novello, 1964), Hymn 318.
21. Nachman of Bratzlav – see *Heart of Prayer* (op. cit.), p. 32.
22. Fred Kaan (1929–) – see *Hymns and Psalms* (op. cit.), Hymn 412.
23. Geoffrey Anketell Studdert–Kennedy (1883–1929) – see *Hymns and Psalms* (op. cit.), Hymn 631.
24. Laurence Housman, 'Love the Tempter' – see *The Oxford Book of English Mystical Verse* (op. cit.), pp. 491–2.
25. Charles Wesley – see *Hymns and Psalms* (op. cit.), Hymn 795.

Week 3

Week 4

Monday

You are my fortress, my loving God.

~ Psalm 59:17 ~

PRAISE

God is exalted in his power.
Who is a teacher like him?
Who has prescribed his ways for him?
Or said to him, 'You have done wrong?'
Remember to extol his work,
which men have praised in song.
All mankind has seen it;
men gaze on it from afar.
How great is God – beyond our understanding!
The number of his years is past finding out.

~ Job 36:22–6 ~

Birth, whenever it occurs, to
Human hearts brings thoughts of sweetness –
Not yet do shades of gloom undo
The pure alloy of innocence
That to the child of every hue
Speaks life. In Bethlehem of
Old a babe was born that unto
Outward eyes provoked such a troth.
But those, with eyes to see beneath
Th' external form, a visage deep
Espied – that to the beingness
Of Being expression gave. Less
Than the Ultimate perhaps but more!
Transcendent love in mortal core!

I praise you, Lord, for all births. For wherever they occur, however unpromising the circumstances, they evoke the mystery of life.

I praise you for my own birth, and for the mystery of my life which is still ongoing.

I praise you for the Lord's birth in Bethlehem. I praise you for the child Jesus, so humbly at the mercy of others.

I praise you for the risen Christ, so humbly at the mercy of human free will, and of servants to do his work.

I praise you for your divine condescension and humility, Sovereign God!

THANKS

We believe in the one High God, who out of love created the beautiful world and everything good in it. He created man and woman, and wanted them to be happy in the world. God loves the world and every nation and tribe on the earth. We have known this High God in the darkness, and now we know him in the light. God promised in the book of his word, the bible, that he would save the world and all the nations and tribes.

We believe that God made good his promise by sending his son, Jesus Christ, a man in the flesh, a Jew by tribe, born poor in a little village, who left his home and was always on safari doing good, curing people by the power of God, teaching about God and humankind, showing that the meaning of religion is love. He was rejected by his people, tortured, nailed hands and feet to a cross, and died. He lay buried in the grave but the hyenas did not touch him, and on the third day he rose from the grave. He ascended to the skies. He is the Lord.

We believe that all our sins are forgiven through him. All who have faith in him must be sorry for their sins, be baptised in the Holy Spirit of God, live the rules of love, and share the bread together in love, to announce the Good News to others until Jesus comes again. We are waiting for him. He is alive. He lives. This we believe. Amen.

~ Masai Creed[1] ~

SELF-EXAMINATION AND FORGIVENESS

Batter my heart, three-person'd God; for, you
As yet but knock, breathe, shine, and seek to mend;
That I may rise, and stand, o'erthrow me, and bend
Your force, to break, blow, burn and make me new.
I, like an usurp'd town, to another due,
Labour to admit you, but Oh, to no end,
Reason your viceroy in me, me should defend,
But is captiv'd, and proves weak or untrue.
Yet dearly I love you, and would be loved fain,
But am betroth'd unto your enemy:
Divorce me, untie, or break that knot again,

Week 4

Take me to you, imprison me, for I
Except you enthral me, never shall be free,
Nor ever chaste, except you ravish me.

~ John Donne[2] ~

I thank you, Lord, for your forgiveness that makes me free. You have taken my past stains, shameful memories, conscious guilts, and known failings and forgiven me for them. Help me daily to know your forgiveness for unconscious traumas and hidden shortcomings. Help your peace to grow in me, even as, in following you, I realise a deepening need for your forgiveness.

Sufficient unto each day is the forgiveness thereof. I thank you for present forgiveness and rejoice in it.

MEDITATION

She gave birth to her first born, a son. She wrapped him in cloths and placed him in a manger.

~ Luke 2:7 ~

When a Samaritan woman came to draw water, Jesus said to her, 'Will you give me a drink?'

~ John 4:7 ~

When the disciples heard this, they fell face down to the ground, terrified. But Jesus came and touched them, 'Get up,' he said. 'Don't be afraid.' When they looked up, they saw no-one except Jesus.

~ Matthew 17:6–8 ~

I am no longer worthy to be called your son; make me like one of your hired men.

~ Luke 15:21 ~

I no longer call you servants, because a servant does not know his master's business. Instead I have called your friends.

~ John 15:15 ~

I am my lover's and my lover is mine.

~ Song of Songs 6:3 ~

Our relationship with God can take many different forms. We look at some of them briefly now. In imagination we experience each different kind of relationship.

We are present in Bethlehem. Jesus has been born and clothed. Mary hands him to us. 'Handle him,' she says. 'Rock him. If necessary, change his clothes.' We do so. For the moment, we are the parents. We see how God has condescended to be shown through the medium of a child. We love that child as parents, we love God.

We are by a well in Samaria. We are alone because we have brought upon ourselves a deep loneliness by reason of our conduct. Jesus comes along. He seems to see into us. We expect a sermon, or exhortations, or a silent gift of some water. Suddenly we hear him speak. He says, 'Will you give me some water?' He doesn't need our help, but he asks for it! Unworthy though we feel, we are wanted by God as his helpers.

We are with Jesus and three of his disciples on a mountain. Suddenly he is changed. His face shines like the sun, and his clothes are as white as the light. We and the disciples fall down terrified. We have become so used to his other forms we had forgotten that he could come to us and dazzle us in a vision. Before God's majesty and awe we can only bow down and worship.

We are the prodigal son returned home in shame and penitence. We are a child to our heavenly Father, but we have been lax to the obligations of childhood and have accepted only its privileges. We want to make amends even if it means becoming a hired labourer. As we try to say this, our Father puts his arms around us and kisses us. We see what his fatherhood means and we honour and love him. We embrace him as a father.

We have looked upon God as our master. We were his servants and we were glad that this was so. Jesus appears before us. 'Servants are alright,' he says, 'but they only obey. They don't have a deep insight into the work they are doing.' 'I no longer call you servants – instead I have called you friends.' We are the friends of God who understand as well as work for his kingdom.

We see Jesus within the room of our heart, indescribably beautiful, his face radiant, his arms outstretched. A deep emotion and desire well up within us. We fly within the space of our heart towards him. We clasp him, and at that moment we seem to disappear. Our spirit has fused with his. We are no longer ourselves. Mystically we love him.

In turn we offer God the adult love of parents, the help of our hands, the awe-struck adoration of our trembling, the love of a child for a parent, the service of servants, the friendship of friends, and the blissful embrace of lovers. In the end, they merge into one another. God's love defies our attempts to classify it. We lack the symbols fully to express our love to God. We just get on and love.

PETITION

This Divine Lord desires only that He may rest in thy soul and may form therein a rich throne of peace, that within thine own heart, by means of internal

Week 4

recollection, and with His heavenly Grace, thou mayest find silence in tumult, solitude in company, light in darkness, forgetfulness in injuries, vigour in despondency, courage in alarms, resistance in temptations, peace in war, and quiet in tribulation.

~ Molinos[3] ~

Deepen, I pray, Lord, my love for you through different symbols and by means of different devotional attitudes. Grant me also a deepening awareness of your love for me and in me. Help me to remember that through my love for you and your love for me I am sent out into the world to serve, and that fruit in actions comes from closeness to you.

PRAYER FOR ACTION

I find it increasingly difficult to conceive of the speed at which we are over-loading Earth's ecosystem. Our numbers have almost doubled in 35 years, and are still growing fast. We are 'consuming' entire regions – forests, grasslands, arable zones – at a pace that should remind us of the image of lily pads extending across a pond. If the pads double in area each day, and if the pond is to be entirely covered in 30 days, on which day is the pond half-covered? Answer: the 29th day . . . We are making a start on the road towards sensible stewardship of our planet. While population grows and grows, and habitats continue to be degraded on every side, there has been an extraordinary outburst of awareness during the past few years. There are hundreds of environmental agencies at official levels, and at grass-roots levels there are thousands of citizen groups, all seeking to come to grips with our problems.

~ *The Gaia Atlas of Planet Management*[4] ~

Lord, I know that we live in a crucial age when the future of life on earth is at stake. Unless my love for you is applied to this endangered earth and your children on it, why have you caused me to be born at this time?

Show me the outworkings of my faith locally and globally. Show me how to think and act sensibly in regard to your earth and your human family.

May the largeness of the task be matched by the largeness of my vision of you and your cosmos to the end that this globe may be the scene of your evolving glory.

CONTEMPLATION

You will keep in perfect peace him whose mind is steadfast.

~ Isaiah 26:3 ~

Week 4

Tuesday

God, you are my refuge and my strength.

PRAISE

I praise you, Lord, for the riches of your being.
You are God.
Your light takes away my darkness; your mercy takes away my offence;
your love redeems me; your energy renews me.
Before I was, you were.
Your greatness and eternity transcend the powers of my mind to grasp.
Yet though I cannot know you as you are in the depth of your glory, I
know you in your effects, and I praise you for them.
You free me from my bonds; you strengthen me when I am weak; you
provide for my needs; you rebuke me when I am complacent; you
challenge me when I am forgetful; you renew my soul.
Within your being you enjoy the fellowship that belongs to the Father,
Son and Holy Spirit. Yet you lavish your fellowship on me, and I
praise you for it.
For your ineffable majesty, for the overflowing creativity of your being,
for your loving intention towards the earth, to all humans, and even
to me,
I praise and adore you, O God!

THANKS

God, our Heavenly Father, we draw near to thee with thankful hearts because
of all thy great love for us. We thank thee most of all for the gift of thy dear Son,
in whom alone we may be one. We are different from one another in race and
language, in material things, in gifts, in opportunities, but each one of us has a
human heart, knowing joy and sorrow, pleasure and pain. We are one in our
need of thy forgiveness, thy strength, thy love; make us one in our common
response to thee, that bound by a common love and freed from selfish aims
we may work for the good of all and the advancement of thy kingdom.

~ Queen Salote of Tonga[5] ~

Week 4

I thank you, Lord, for all your gifts. I am grateful for everyday gifts: for pure water to drink, for a variety of foods to eat, for different kinds of clothes to wear, for a pleasant home. I thank you for the privilege of being born in this dynamic age when all peoples are being drawn together. I thank you for all the persons who help and love me daily. For the inner riches of the spirit, which I have so feebly tapped, and for the deepening promise of your kingdom I offer you my thanks.

Above all I thank you that you have put into my life an inclination to give you thanks. Deepen my desire to give thanks. So may the events to do with my body, mind and spirit be traced back to you and given back to you, the eternal Giver.

SELF-EXAMINATION AND FORGIVENESS

St Peter once: 'Lord, dost Thou wash my feet?'
    Much more I say: Lord, dost Thou stand and knock
    At my closed heart more rugged than a rock,
Bolted and barred, for Thy soft touch unmeet,
Nor garnished nor in any wise made sweet?
    Owls roost within and dancing satyrs mock,
    Lord, I have heard the crowing of the cock
and have not wept: ah, Lord, thou knowest it.
Yet still I hear Thee knocking, still I hear:
    'Open to Me, look on Me eye to eye,
That I may wring thy heart and make it whole;
And teach thee love because I hold thee dear
    And sup with thee in gladness soul with soul,
And sup with thee in glory by and by.'

~ Christina Rossetti[6] ~

I know full well, Lord, that before I turn to seek you, you are already seeking me; before I come to you in confession, you are waiting to forgive me; before I cry in penitence before you, you are already raising me up with joy.

Yet I do turn to seek you, I do confess before you, and I do cry out in penitence.

May I feel now your seeking, forgiving and joyful love in the depths of my heart, even as I know it in the top of my head.

MEDITATION

Now on his way to Jerusalem, Jesus travelled along the border between Samaria and Galilee. As he was going into a village, ten men who had leprosy met him. They stood at a distance and called out in a loud voice, 'Jesus, Master, have pity on us!'

When he saw them, he said, 'Go show yourselves to the priests'. And as they went, they were cleansed.

Week 4

One of them, when he saw he was healed, came back, praising God in a loud voice. He threw himself at Jesus' feet and thanked him – and he was a Samaritan. Jesus asked, 'Were not all ten cleansed? Where are the other nine? Was no-one found to return and give praise to God except this foreigner?' Then he said to him, 'Rise and go; your faith has made you well.'

~ Luke 17:11–19 ~

This story can be reflected on at different levels. In one sense it can be seen as a historical happening; in another sense it can be seen as an allegory of the soul; in a third sense it can be related by analogy to present-day events. In this meditation, I want to concentrate upon the third level of interpretation – this story and the modern world – with a backward glance to the second allegorical level. For by analogy the leprosy of this story is not far from the AIDS of today.

The cry of the ten lepers, 'Have pity on us,' pulls at our heartstrings. They of all people seemed to be in need of pity. Their disease was felt to be incurable. They had probably tried to hide it. They had probably tried to isolate themselves as far as possible from normal contacts in order to keep their secret. Now they were found out. They had to live in the open, but separate from society, and the only way they could contact others was by standing at a distance and calling out in a loud voice. To make matters worse others tended to see their disease, and they probably saw it themselves, as a punishment for their wrongdoings.

The situation of sufferers from AIDS also pulls at our heartstrings. With adjustments for the increased compassion and understanding of our day, it is sometimes true that they too feel that AIDS is incurable; they too sometimes try to hide it; they too sometimes try to isolate themselves in order to keep their secret; they too, and society with them, sometimes see their disease as a punishment for their wrongdoings. Their implicit cry is 'Have pity on us.'

Leprosy is now treatable, although it is estimated that only 3 out of 15 million lepers are receiving treatment. It is reasonably certain that AIDS will eventually be treatable as well. Let us look at two implications arising out of this. Leprosy and AIDS are medical problems demanding from us imaginative love, sympathy and counsel as well as medical skill on the Christ principle that we are called to mourn with the mourner, comfort the sorrowful, and help those in distress. We give our prayers, our money, and our insight to provide mobile clinics and hospitals and research to the end that AIDS as well as leprosy may be 'cracked' and deprived of its sting. 'Go, with our blessing, to the modern-day priests, the doctors,' we say, 'and take advantage of their God-given talents.' We crave for them too a deeper gift: that if and when they are healed they may praise God and give thanks. For healing is not just of the body, it is also of the whole person. It is being able to forgive oneself for one's own wrongdoings and

Week 4

to forgive others the slights they have heaped upon us. It is to know the healing life of God in the soul as well as in the body.

And at this point we are no longer onlookers. For although we may not know leprosy or AIDS in our body, we cannot hide from ourselves the fact that we suffer from a leprosy or AIDS of the soul. We too have cried out, 'Jesus, Master, have pity on us!' We too, having been cleansed, have neglected to return and give praise to God. We, too, have forgotten our mortality, our dependence and our stewardship. Although we cannot normally know leprosy or AIDS in a bodily sense, in a general sense we can identify with our brothers and sisters with leprosy and AIDS. It is no longer just a question of 'them with leprosy and AIDS'; we can now say 'we all with leprosy and AIDS'.

As daily we go back and praise God, and throw ourselves at Jesus's feet and thank him, we hear the words, 'Rise and go; your faith has made you well.' We also recognise the truth of Wesley's words, 'Go not just to those who need you but to those who need you most.' As we own and through God's grace deal with the secret leprosy and AIDS of our own soul, we are sent out to grapple compassionately and imaginatively with the overt leprosy and AIDS in the world in the name of him who, while knowing no sin, yet became sin for our sakes.

PETITION

To desert fellahin and royal
Heirs you open wide your gates
O lordly realm! Your courtiers tell
Of wounds, and thorns, and pain, and weights
That burden still the secret life
Of Him who hosts your simple court,
While from your guests is hidden His strife
Concealed in loving service kindly wrought.
How enter we this paradise
Of love so purely given? What price
Is fit for such a place? No walls
It builds to bar our way. It falls
To simple faith that to the world
Of spirit cries, 'I come with heart unfurled!'

O Lord, I come with heart unfurled. Open the gates of your kingdom to me. Grant that I may receive its pain as well as its grandeur, its challenge as well as its solace, its openness to the world as well as its halls of paradise, its lamb slain from the foundation of the world as well as its risen Lord. For yours is the pain and the power and the glory, forever and ever.

Week 4

PRAYER FOR ACTION

Is not the work done? Nay, for still the Scars
Are open; still Earth's Pain stands deified,
With Arms spread wide:
And still, like falling stars,
Its Blood-drops strike the doorposts, where abide
The watchers with the Bride,
To wait the final coming of their kin,
And hear the sound of kingdoms gathering in.

While Earth wears wounds, still must Christ's Wounds remain,
Whom Love made Life, and of Whom Life made Pain,
And of Whom Pain made Death.
No breath,
Without Him, sorrow draws; no feet
Wax weary, and no hands hard labour bear,
But He doth wear
The travail and the heat:
Also, for all things perishing, He saith,
'MY grief, MY pain, MY death.'

O kindred Constellation of bright stars,
Ye shall not last for aye!
Far off there dawns a comfortable day
Of healing for those Scars:
When, faint in glory, shall be wiped away
Each planetary fire,
Now, all the aching way the balm of Earth's desire!

~ Laurence Housman [7] ~

Three Global Commandments

Love the global God of all with all your heart, and soul, and mind and strength.

Love the beautiful planet on which we live, and treat it with deep care and concern.

Love the human brothers and sisters who live on it as you love yourself.

Grant to me and to each of us, O Lord, a vision of the world as it might be, and a deep love for the world as it is. May my vision of the world to come be grounded in my present service in the world, and may my present service illuminate the world to come – for both are gathered up within the folds of the garments of your kingdom.

CONTEMPLATION

Do not be discouraged,
for the Lord your God will be with you wherever you go.

~ Joshua 1:9 ~

Week 4

Wednesday

APPROACH

The kingdom of God is within you.

~ Luke 17:21 ~

PRAISE

1. *O God, thy being who can sound?*
   Thee to perfection who can know?
   O height immense! No words are found
   Thy countless attributes to show.

2. *Unfathomable depths thou art!*
   O plunge me in thy mercy's sea;
   Void of true wisdom is my heart:
   With love embrace and cover me.

3. *Eternity thy fountain was,*
   Which, like thee, no beginning knew;
   Thou wast ere time began his race,
   Ere gloved with stars the ethereal blue.

4. *Unchangeable, all-perfect Lord,*
   Essential life's unbounded sea,
   What lives and moves lives by thy word;
   It lives, and moves, and is from thee.

5. *Parent of good, thy bounteous hand*
   Incessant blessings down distils.
   And all in air, or sea, or land
   With plenteous food and gladness fills.

Week 4

6. *Greatness unspeakable is thine,*
   Thou sun, whose undiminished ray,
   When short-lived worlds are lost, shall shine
   When earth and heav'n are fled away.

~ Ernst Lange[8] ~

God our Father, who anticipated my birth, who loves me now, who prepares a place for me, give me a deeper awareness of who I am and of whose I am, and help me to praise you in all the circumstances of my life, until the time comes when the whole world accepts the comfort and the challenge of your everlasting arms.

THANKS

It fortifies my soul to know
That, though I perish, Truth is so;
That, howso'er I stray and range,
Whate'er I do, Thou dost not change.
I steadier step when I recall
That, if I slip, Thou dost not fall.

~ A. H. Clough[9] ~

SELF-EXAMINATION AND FORGIVENESS

Lord, you love me with an everlasting love, and are ready to meet my needs before I mention them to you. Come to me with your forgiveness.

Forgive me for my sins of commission: for being ready to react with hatred rather than love, for having enemies and taking advantage of them, for hasty words, for unkind judgements, for insidious remarks, for turning my back on the cross.

Forgive me for my sins of omission: for those in need whom I have not helped, for those who are hungry because I was too blind to see their hunger, for those discriminated against whom I have not defended, for those forlorn or angry or broken because I have stood on one side.

Forgive me for my sins of anxiety: for worry about what I did in the past, for worry about what will happen tomorrow, for worry about what people think of me, for anxious care that makes me selfish.

Forgive me for my sins of timidity: that I expect so little from you who offer me so much, that I am content with drops from your ocean of love, that I venture so little in fellowship with others.

Forgive me, O Lord! Help me to see that the past is gone forever. I repent of what is gone and I receive your forgiveness. Today is a new day

Week 4

and I hear you saying 'This is the first day of your life!' I accept this day gladly and I offer it to you.

MEDITATION

And beginning with Moses and all the prophets, he explained to them what was said in all the Scriptures concerning himself.

As they approached the village to which they were going, Jesus acted as if he were going further. But they urged him strongly, 'Stay with us, for it is nearly evening; the day is almost over.' So he went in to stay with them.

When he was at the table with them, he took bread, gave thanks, broke it and began to give it to them. Then their eyes were opened and they recognised him, and he disappeared from their sight. They asked each other, 'Were not our hearts burning within us while he talked with us on the road and opened the Scriptures to us?'

~ Luke 24:27–32 ~

The risen Christ is always with us. We imagine him walking along the road to Emmaus with two disciples. We see their animated conversation. We see them invite him to eat with them. We see him handing the bread round to them. We see their recognition of who he is, and Lo! He is gone. They say to one another: 'Were not our hearts burning within us while he talked with us on the road?' Perhaps they are reading back their present realisation of who he is into their past experience. After all on the road they had been concerned and preoccupied. We share both their perplexity and their burning hearts. How can we know the risen Christ with us at all, and how can we know him with us all the time?

We see the Christ who vanished from the table of the two disciples coming and sitting with us in this room. He is here anyway; by the use of our imagination we can make him real. We picture him wearing his outdoor clothes, or we picture him as a general presence. We say to him, 'Lord, you are here.' We share with him our surface and hidden thoughts. The content varies according to person and place. Perhaps we tell him our experiences of yesterday, our equivalent of the road to Emmaus they walked along: of the people we met, the decisions we made, the thoughts we had, the plans we envisaged. We tell him too about what will happen today: the people we are likely to meet, the work we have to do, the projects we have in hand. We share them with him, and we listen to his comments upon our life ahead. We hear him say, 'Now go out and I will be with you' – and he vanishes from our sight. He was there before we visualised him in the first place; he remains there after we seem to see him disappear.

During the day we see him near us at different times. We say, 'Hello, Lord', or we smile, or we just look. We listen to him, or we see his reaction. Perhaps our heart burns within us. More and more we open up our spiritual

Week 4

eye to his presence, and we recall what is already true namely that he is present with us. We may be aware of him also in other people but our concern at this point is above all with his unseen presence. As time goes on we become better able to practise the presence of the risen Lord. And as we look back upon the past day with him, and look forward to the next day with him, our unseen guest becomes more and more our spiritually seen guest. For nothing can separate us from his presence except our unwillingness to acknowledge it.

PETITION

1. *Lead, kindly Light, amid the encircling gloom,*
   Lead thou me on;
   The night is dark, and I am far from home,
   Lead thou me on.
   Keep thou my feet, I do not ask to see
   The distant scene, one step enough for me.

2. *I was not ever thus, nor prayed that thou*
   Should'st lead me on;
   I loved to choose and see my path; but now
   Lead thou me on.
   I loved the garish day, and, spite of fears,
   Pride rules my will: remember not past years.

3. *So long thy power hath blessed me, sure it still*
   Will lead me on,
   O'er moor and fen, o'er crag and torrent, till
   The night is gone;
   And with the morn those angel faces smile,
   Which I have loved long since, and lost awhile.

~ John Henry Newman[10] ~

PRAYER FOR ACTION

Ode to Hope

1. *Hope, Ideal of those who labour*
   For a world bereft of strife,
   You our spur and hidden savour –
   How shall we despair of life?
   When the storms of doubt assail us,
   When our fellows faint and fail,
   Pricked by you, new zeal reviving,
   Press we onward and prevail.

Week 4

2. *Hope, O Hope, supreme Inspirer,*
   Buffeted by holocaust,
   Tempted by the great denier,
   Gloom, to ponder all as lost.
   Deep within both hearts and nations
   Working veiled and surging long,
   Faith and love your near relations,
   Raise you still the triumph-song!

3. *Forgive, O Hope, our weak endeavour*
   To descry your victory,
   Overlook our timeous failure
   To o'erfly our misery.
   Prison, torture, death and hunger
   Scorn your banner, mute your lay;
   Wisdom, beauty, honour, valour,
   Height and depth your form display!

4. *Hope, renewing salve, how potent*
   Is your power to fill us still
   With the soul-enlivening moment
   That transports us, 'gainst our will,
   'Yond the constraints of the body,
   'Neath the shackles of the mind,
   To a realm astride earth's glory
   Human yet in ilk and kind.

5. *Hope, elating Gift, that ever*
   Goes before us, Beacon bright,
   Daily toil and quickening leisure
   Find new meaning in your light!
   Calm and sorrow, gain and failure,
   In your beams perspective find!
   Matchless Norm, ennobling Treasure,
   Transcendent Guide of humankind!

6. *Wherefore, as the world we gather*
   Like a mother to our breast,
   Can we guidance from you filter
   Turmoil to transform to rest?
   Human voices speak your accent
   Out of every race and tongue:
   'Each to all, Hope's envoys sent
   We are,' with joy sounds forth their song.

7. *May we, to cry your praise, mouths/hearts*
   In simmering hundreds but possess!
   How can we hymn you, glorious Hope,

Week 4

Your garb to adorn, your joy to bless?
As much of self as we do know
To you we grant, poor as we are,
May we into your being grow
Herald divine come from afar!

8. *Hope, the Name beyond all others,*
   Soaring Sound, ecstatic Pause!
   Sisters are we all and brothers
   Hand in hand to plead your cause!
   Ravished are our souls when livened
   By your awe that makes us one,
   Never shall our vigil slacken
   Till your bliss on earth be won!

CONTEMPLATION

Nothing in all creation will be able to separate us from the love of God.

~ Romans 8:39 ~

Week 4

Thursday

APPROACH

Help me, O Lord, to go beyond my thoughts, good as well as bad, into the living flame of your presence.

PRAISE

We praise you, O God. We acknowledge you to be the Lord. We adore you for what you are.

And yet we can only worship as much of yourself as we know with as much of ourself as we know. You are higher than our minds can fully grasp; you are nearer than our hearts can fully know; you are deeper than our spirits can fully realise.

We praise you for as much of yourself as we do know. We love because you first loved us; we approach you because you set in our hearts a hunger for you; we come with joy because you have already forgiven us; we realise your presence because your spirit already abides within us.

Although through our blindness we know so little of you, grant the intentions of our hearts which cry out: O for a thousand tongues to praise my God! O for a thousand eyes to glorify his beauty! O for a thousand hands to raise in adoration!

Receive me, O Lord, poor as I am, and grant that as I come to know myself more dearly, I may come to love and worship you more dearly. For all your being, known or unknown; for all your mercies, known or unknown; for intimations of your glory; for glimpses of your indwelling radiance – we praise your holy name, O Lord!

THANKS

Eternal God, whose grace is inexhaustible, I give you thanks for your love that has gone before me and beckoned me on. I thank you for the unique life you have entrusted to me, and for the free will you have offered me. I thank you for the beauty of the world that is the setting of that life, and for the family and friends among whom it is lived.

I thank you for your light, which has shone before especially in times of darkness, for your strength, which has beckoned especially in times of

Week 4

affliction, for your joy, which has prevailed especially in times of dryness, for your peace, which has been deeper than the trials that have led me on.

For all your love, and for the abundance of your grace, I give you thanks, O Lord!

SELF-EXAMINATION

How much of my life is inward and private? How much of my conversation is the recycling of what is seen on the television, heard on the radio, read in the newspaper, or heard from the neighbours? Do I have a life with you, O Lord? Do I have a life that is mine, not in the self-seeking sense but as an abiding in you? How often have you called and I have not heard, been present and I have not known, remembered and I have not registered your grace?

From the depths of my despair
    I call to you, Lord.
Hear my cry, O Lord;
    listen to my call for help!
If you kept a record of our sins,
    who could escape being condemned?
But you forgive us,
    so that we should stand in awe of you.

I wait eagerly for the Lord's help,
    and in his word I trust.
I wait for the Lord
    more eagerly than watchmen wait for the dawn –
    than watchmen wait for the dawn.

Israel, trust in the Lord,
    because his love is constant
    and he is always willing to save.
He will save his people Israel
    from all their sins.

~ Psalm 130 ~

MEDITATION

Where are you, O Lord? I search for you and you do not seem to be there.

Meanwhile the business of the day begins. At the end of a lecture, a female student asks a question. Something lies behind it and we talk. She tells of a broken marriage and a broken heart lying beyond her intellectual problems. It takes time, but she goes away with some new perspectives. But where are you, Lord?

At the end of a committee, a colleague chats. We go for coffee. He too has known a broken marriage. After years of trauma he has come through

Week 4

it and is married again and a stronger person. Time has passed again, but he says it helped him to talk and he goes away rejoicing. But where are you, Lord?

Another student comes in to discuss an essay. Discussion passes beyond the essay to hidden thoughts of failure and worse. It takes time, but comfort is given and further sources of help are opened up to him as he goes away. But where are you, Lord?

Some words float across the screen of the mind: inasmuch as you did it to the least of these, my little ones, you did it to me. Some images float across the mind as well: a female student who asked a question at a lecture, a colleague who chatted after a committee, a male student who came to discuss an essay.

O Lord, I sought earnestly to find you, but all the time you were finding me through people and events in my life!

PETITION

1. *Father of everlasting grace,*
   Thy goodness and thy truth we praise,
      Thy goodness and thy truth we prove;
   Thou hast, in honour of thy Son,
   The gift unspeakable sent down,
      The Spirit of life, and power, and love.

2. *Send us the Spirit of thy Son*
   To make the depths of Godhead known,
      To make us share the life divine;
   Send him the sprinkled blood t'apply,
   Send him our souls to sanctify,
      And show and seal us ever thine.

3. *So shall we pray, and never cease,*
   So shall we thankfully confess
      Thy wisdom, truth, and power, and love,
   With joy unspeakable adore,
   And bless, and praise thee evermore,
      And serve thee as thy hosts above.

4. *Till added to that heavenly choir*
   We raise our songs of triumph higher,
      And praise thee in a bolder strain,
   Out-soar the firstborn seraph's flight,
   And sing, with all our friends in light,
      Thy everlasting love to man.

~ Charles Wesley[11] ~

Week 4

PRAYER FOR ACTION

A recent report talks about there being up to fifty million refugees in the world today. Fifty million? Even if it is exaggerated, even if there were only a thousand, it is a challenge and stimulus to our prayers, it is a challenge and stimulus to us as human beings alive in the world today.

1. *Guardian of those in need and Guard*
   Of those who seek a world renewed;
   You succour those whose lives are hard,
   You challenge status unreviewed!
   Your cross our stay, your life our guide,
   Help us in your will to abide!

2. *Held in your everlasting arms,*
   We will not move from your intent;
   Upheld by you amidst all harms,
   To all your children we are sent!
   The whole wide earth to love restored,
   Becomes our common goal, O Lord!

Help us to enter, O Lord, through the creative imagination of prayer, into the situation of our brothers and sisters who are refugees.

Here is one – bewildered, hungry, poor and weak. Some family are lost forever as far as this earth is concerned; others are present, but how will they live? Here is one forced to rely on charity who has never done so before. Here is one cast away in a strange land. Here is one in whose mind there wells up the thought, what have I done that it should happen to me and my loved ones? Here is one who seeks to cling on to the seeds of hope but is tempted to give way to despair.

Another seeks to help. She is overworked and tired. She is forced to choose between those who will get more and those who will get less, for there is not enough to satisfy everyone. Feelings of guilt arise: why should I have so much and eat so well at night when they have so little? There is anger at the callousness of those who do not want to know.

We do not know all the reasons, Lord. Perhaps there are many: the malice of evil persons, the lack of thought on the part of others, the misuse of free will, the pain pangs of a world in process of rapid change.

Grant us the gift of compassion, O Lord. Give us knowledge of the situation of our brothers and sisters who are refugees, a willingness to help directly any who may be nearby, an imaginative love for individuals as well as groups, a compassionate anger for change.

Grant us compassion for ourselves. We did not ask to be born as non-refugees, but we also know that we cannot escape some responsibility for

Week 4

their plight. We know too that we ourselves are refugees and yet we do not know it. Our material security has blinded us to the fact that we live on this earth as pilgrims, not as those who will enjoy it forever. We pray for our brothers and sisters in our mutual need.

Save us from complacency, O Lord. Because we know that human beings do not live by bread alone and that the Son of Man had nowhere to lay his head, spur us by this very knowledge to greater efforts on behalf of those who do not have bread or anywhere to lay their head. Move us to action, O Lord!

CONTEMPLATION

Lord Jesus Christ, have mercy upon us.

Week 4

Friday

Offer your bodies as living sacrifices, holy and pleasing to God – this is your spiritual act of worship.

–~ Romans 12:1 ~–

PRAISE

If music be the source of hope
Play on, O Muse! Extend your sound
Throughout the firmament! Nor pope,
Nor priest, nor commissar, the wound
Of angst can overcome so sure
As you, who by your echo pure
Dost energise the heart – that o'er
The slough of fear it high may soar!
Our soul from pain how do you free?
'Tis hid from us! Yet this we know,
That through your rhythms that in us flow,
Our grief becomes expectancy!

1. *Poignant world, joyful world,*
   On the cross lies unfurled
   You whom heav'n and earth adore
   Dying, living evermore
   Loving in agony!

2. *Doleful world, blissful world,*
   Through the universe is hurled
   Mercy ignited by nails sublime
   Streaming through the fold of time
   From you, O Calvary!

3. *Mournful world, graceful world,*
   With cruel thorns your head is curled!

Week 4

Broken on that fateful beam,
Piercing all with love supreme,
You hang, O Son of God!

4. *Wounded world, healing world,*
   Tyrants ever swords have twirled,
   Vain their pomp, their cause is lost,
   Rejoice earth, shout you heavenly host,
   Christ the Saviour reigns!

I praise you, Lord, for your own being. I praise you too for the gift of silence in which to recognise your being.

I praise you for the silence of heart in which your Holy Spirit can gently speak. I praise you for the silence in which I can know myself, and for the silence in which I can know you.

I praise you for the silence that tends to humility and the silence that tends to confidence; for the silence that communicates without words and the silence that hears without voices; for the silence of faith and the silence of love.

I praise you for the still, small voice of your silence that fixes me in wisdom and peace.

I praise you above all for the ability to be silent. Grant that when the whisper of your grace is uttered I may not be slow to hear.

To your name be the honour and glory.

THANKS

I have loved to hear my Lord spoken of, and wherever I have seen the print of his shoe in the earth, there I have coveted to set my foot too. His name has been to me as a civet-box, yea, sweeter than all perfumes. His voice to me has been most sweet, and his countenance I have more desired than they that have most desired the light of the sun. His words I did use to gather my food, and for antidotes against my faintings. He has held me, and hath kept me from mine iniquities; yea, my steps hath he strengthened in His way.

~ John Bunyan[12] ~

I thank you, Lord, for your many gifts. I thank you for the glory of sight; I thank you for the pearl of hearing; I thank you for the blessing of speech; I thank you for the soothing qualities of the breath I take.

There is so much to thank you for, Lord, but at this time I thank you for the gift of yourself: for your life on earth, for your service to others, for your words of teaching, for the glory of your cross, for your triumph over death, for your presence with me now ascendant, triumphant and yet offering to wash my feet.

For the abundance of your gifts, and for yourself, I thank you, Lord.

Week 4

SELF-EXAMINATION AND FORGIVENESS

1. *One who is all unfit to count*
   As scholar in thy school,
   Thou of thy love hast named a friend –
   O kindness wonderful!

2. *So weak am I, O gracious Lord,*
   So all unworthy thee,
   That e'en the dust upon thy feet
   Outweighs me utterly.

3. *Thou dwellest in unshadowed light,*
   All sin and shame above –
   That thou shouldst bear our sin and shame,
   How can I tell such love?

4. *Ah, did not he the heavenly throne*
   A little thing esteem,
   And not unworthy for my sake
   A mortal body deem?

5. *When in his flesh they drove the nails,*
   Did he not all endure?
   What name is there to fit a life
   So patient and so pure?

6. *So, love itself in human form,*
   For love of me he came;
   I cannot look upon his face
   For shame, for bitter shame.

7. *If there is aught of worth in me,*
   It comes from thee alone;
   Then keep me safe, for so, O Lord,
   Thou keepest but thine own.

~ N. V. Tilak[13] ~

MEDITATION

Today, I bring to mind the seven words of the cross. I do so through the medium of silence rather than words.

I sit comfortably in my chair, with my feet on the floor and my back firm. I gradually become aware of my breathing. I observe my breathing. I rejoice in it. When I am comfortable with my breath coming in and out I attach words to my outbreath and my inbreath. As I breathe out I repeat silently 'I love God', and as I breathe in I repeat silently 'God loves me.'

Week 4

This repetition of 'I love God, God loves me' becomes part of the breathing process. I then change it to 'I love you' and 'You love me' so that the repetition of 'I love you, you love me' becomes part of my breathing process.

Against this background I call to mind the seven words from the cross. If my mind strays, it strays back to the breathing process of 'I love you, you love me.' I see Christ on the cross. I imagine him there. I am not mainly concerning with his pain (that would be another exercise) but with himself on the cross and the words he says. I take each one of Christ's words and I see him saying it. I see him repeating it ten times or more. I watch him, and I let the words sink in. In between I revert back to the awareness of my breathing 'I love you, you love me' before passing on to the next word. I begin and carry through the meditation:

'Father, forgive them, for they do not know what they are doing.'

~ Luke 23:34 ~

'I tell you the truth, today you will be with me in paradise.'

~ Luke 23:43 ~

'Dear woman, here is your son,'
... and to John, 'Here is your mother.'

~ John 19:26–7 ~

'My God, my God, why have you forsaken me?'

~ Matthew 27:45; Mark 15:34 ~

'I am thirsty.'

~ John 19:28 ~

'It is finished.'

~ John 19:30 ~

'Father, into your hands I commit my spirit.'

~ Luke 23:46 ~

I revert back to 'I love you, you love me' for a short time. I return from the cross and sense the risen Christ in me. I say consciously, 'I love you, you love me.' I sense him saying 'I love you, you love me.'

PETITION

Lord, may I love all your creation, the whole and every grain of sand in it. May I love every leaf, every ray of your light. May I love the animals: you have given them the rudiments of thought and joy untroubled. Let me not trouble it, let me not harass them, let me not deprive them of their happiness, let me not work against your intent. For I acknowledge unto you that all is like an ocean, all is flowing and blending, and that to withhold any measure of love from anything in your universe is to withhold that same measure from you.

~ Adapted from Dostoievsky[14] ~

Week 4

God our Father, may the peace and love which flows out from the cross everywhere and to all eternity flow into my heart now that I may cry, 'My Lord, and my God.'

PRAYER FOR ACTION

Ode to Peace

1. *Peace, among all gifts the treasure*
   Sought by most on planet earth,
   Firm in duty and in leisure,
   How can we explain your dearth?
   Efforts to attain your merit
   Plenteous are from sea to shore,
   Yet the riches of your spirit
   Taunt our poverty the more.

2. *Peace, O ravishing Bewitcher,*
   We must know you, or we die!
   Far beyond all earthly pleasure
   Shines your rapture in the sky!
   Higher than the highest mountain,
   Brighter than the whitest pearl,
   Pure alloy, cascading fountain,
   The travails of our heart unfurl!

3. *When among our friends we gather,*
   When before our God we pray,
   Of your glory is our converse,
   May you ever with us stay!
   For the bonds that make us human
   And our certainties divine
   From your energies are woven,
   Through your prism glint sublime!

4. *Priceless goal of all our striving*
   How can we extol your worth?
   End right now our aching pining,
   In our soul begin your birth.
   May your kingdom, like a flower,
   Bud within us while we breathe,
   That our very bones a choir,
   A choir of fragrance may breath!

Week 4

5. *In our mind the whole world gathers,*
   Summoned instant by your grace,
   All men come to us as brothers –
   Sisters too of every race,
   Cry they with adoring wonder,
   Tear-clad, vibrant in their joy,
   'May all humans stay for ever
   In this peace that doth not cloy.'

6. *Is this ecstasy a feeling*
   Substanceless that comes and goes?
   Maybe so, yet overarching
   Hot emotion's ebbs and flows
   Is a thread of life eternal,
   Streaming through the firmament,
   Mirroring the light supernal
   That from God to earth is sent.

7. *Peace, O Peace, thou wondrous Jewel,*
   Glorious angel winging high,
   We with human voices stumble
   To extol your liberty!
   Deep within us hangs a ladder
   Linking humans, God and earth,
   Sure we are it will not falter,
   You its surety, you its birth.

8. *Therefore, Peace, our tongues we loosen*
   To give vent to shouts of praise.
   Likewise, too, our hearts we open
   To adore you all our days.
   Healer, Helper, Bard of Gladness,
   Firm Defender, Joyous Swain,
   Herald of a time when sadness
   Gone will be along with pain!

It is not our job to master everything and to be everywhere, but to do what we can with the years that are ours, restoring the fields that are given to us and putting right what is in our power, so that those who follow may have a better earth to tend and a better world to enjoy. The weather that will be theirs and the use they make of it is not our prerogative. Let us be in peace.

CONTEMPLATION

I am with you always, to the very end of the age.

~ Matthew 28:20 ~

Week 4

Saturday

APPROACH

God's Spirit is seated in my heart and in the hearts of all.

PRAISE

I praise you, O God, for your majesty which rules me, for your compassion which has mercy on me, for your love which envelops me, for your wisdom which enlightens me, for your immensity which enfolds me, for your serenity which calms me, for your Spirit which challenges me, for your beauty which kindles my imagination, and for your mercy which redeems me.

I love Thee with two loves, love of my happiness, and perfect love to love Thee as is Thy due. My selfish love is that I do naught but think on Thee, excluding all beside; but that purest love, which is Thy due, is that the veils which hide Thee fall and I gaze on Thee, no praise to me in either this or that, nay Thine the praise for both that love and this.

~ Rabi'a[15] ~

THANKS

1. *Hail, Father, Son and Holy Ghost,*
   One God in Persons Three;
   Of thee we make our joyful boast,
   Our songs we make of thee.

2. *Thou neither canst be felt or seen;*
   Thou art a spirit pure;
   Thou from eternity hast been,
   And always shalt endure.

3. *Present alike in every place,*
   Thy Godhead we adore;
   Beyond the bounds of time and space
   Thou dwell'st for evermore.

4. *In wisdom infinite thou art,*
    Thine eye doth all things see.
    And every thought of every heart
    Is fully known to thee.

5. *Whate'er thou wilt in earth below*
    Thou dost in heaven above;
    But chiefly we rejoice to know
    The Almighty God of love.

6. *Thou lov'st whate'er thy hands have made;*
    Thy goodness we rehearse,
    In shining characters displayed
    Throughout our universe.

7. *Mercy, with love, and endless grace*
    O'er all thy works doth reign;
    But mostly thou delight'st to bless
    Thy favourite creature, man.

8. *Wherefore let every creature give*
    To thee the praise designed;
    But chiefly, Lord, the thanks receive,
    The hearts of all mankind.

~ Charles Wesley[16] ~

Lord, I thank you for this day with its predictable situations and its glorious uncertainties. I thank you for the people I know I will meet, and for the other people who will cross my path. I thank you that you go before me.

Use their gifts and their contributions to illuminate my path – those people who will be my touchstones for living today. Use my gifts as well – those I am comfortable with, and my fantasies, my desires, and my aggressions, which I am not so comfortable with – that this day may be unique in its opportunities for growth, its occasions for repentance, and its possibilities for deeper insight into who you are, who I am, and who my fellows are.

SELF-EXAMINATION AND FORGIVENESS

O Christ who holds the open gate,
O Christ who drives the furrow straight,
O Christ, the plough, O Christ, the laughter
Of holy white birds flying after,

Week 4

Lo, all my heart's field red and torn,
And Thou wilt bring the young green corn
The young green corn divinely springing,
The young green corn for ever singing;
And when the field is fresh and fair
Thy blessèd feet shall glitter there.
And we will walk the weeded field,
And tell the golden harvest's yield,
The corn that makes the holy bread
By which the soul of man is fed,
The holy bread, the food unpriced,
Thy everlasting mercy, Christ.

~ John Masefield [17] ~

O Lord, my God, Light of the blind and Strength of the weak; yea also, Light of those that see and Strength of the strong; hearken unto my soul, and hear it crying out of the depths.

O Lord, help us to turn and seek Thee; for Thou has not forsaken Thy creatures as we have forsaken Thee our creator. Let us turn and seek Thee, for we know Thou art here in our hearts, when we confess to Thee, when we cast ourselves upon Thee, and weep in Thy bosom, after all our rugged ways; and Thou dost gently wipe away out tears, and we weep the more for joy; because Thou, Lord, who madest us, dost re-make and comfort us.

Hear, Lord, my prayer, and grant that I may most entirely love Thee, and do Thou rescue me, O Lord, from every temptation, even unto the end.

~ St Augustine[18] ~

MEDITATION

When Jesus saw the crowd around him, he gave orders to cross to the other side of the lake. Then a teacher of the law came to him and said, 'Teacher, I will follow you wherever you go'. Jesus replied, 'Foxes have holes and birds of the air have nests, but the Son of Man has nowhere to lay his head'. Another disciple said to him, 'Lord, first let me go and bury my father'. But Jesus told him, 'Follow me, and let the dead bury their own dead'.

~ Matthew 8:18–22 ~

As you and I meditate upon this passage, in all probability we are doing so within a reasonably pleasant home. It is also probable that the Jesus who spoke these words spent his early life within a pleasant and secure home in Nazareth. As we ponder this challenge to become followers of the Way, we do so as those who have a home that we can 'forsake'.

We make a leap of imagination into some situations of homelessness at the beginning of the 21st century. Here is a family in South America. Their rural plot is too small to feed a growing family so they move to the city. Their dream of plenty turns out to be a pavement home. Their

Week 4

practical problems are many. The father is tempted to steal or to leave. The mother is tempted to prostitution or to alcohol. The children, who live on the street by day, are tempted to separate from their family and become street children permanently.

Here is another family in an African city who are determined to stay together. Their home is in a shanty town. The rain drips through the corrugated iron roof; the open street outside is a sewer; robbers can easily take away what few possessions they have; jobs, health facilities, and education are very hard to obtain; they have next to no money. It is estimated that over half the people in places such as Calcutta and Ibadan, Nigeria, live in squatter camps, and that 7 of the 17 million people of Mexico city do the same. Nor are some western cities, although their problems are much less, bereft of people living in parks, under bridges, and in other open places. Foxes have holes, birds have nests, but many of our fellows have nowhere to lay their head. Admittedly 'stone walls do not a home make', and people do not live by homes alone – but, O God!, how the many other problems of life are compounded by homelessness!

In our meditation eye, we see a vision of a world which is a home for all – where all peoples' needs for housing, food, education, health and jobs are met. A world of mutual help where the poor are aided and encouraged to build houses for themselves. What can I do through prayer, giving, moral persuasion and self-sacrifice to make this more possible?

However, there is another level to home: homes are not just four walls and a roof. Home is where I can find contentment and fulfilment of body, mind and spirit, and help others to find contentment and fulfilment of body, mind and spirit.

Lord, can it be that I have made my home into my god, that satisfaction of my material comforts has become a block to my providential way, that I am eager to follow you, Lord, but not if it means upsetting the routine of my home? 'Teacher, I will follow you wherever you go.' What does that mean, Lord, for me, now?

PETITION

O God, give me strength to be victorious over myself, for nothing may chain me to this life. O guide my spirit, O raise me from these dark depths, that my soul, transported through thy wisdom, may fearlessly struggle upward in fiery flight. For thou alone understandest and canst inspire me.

~ Adapted from Ludwig van Beethoven ~

I pray, Lord, for the imagination and empathy to understand the problem of homelessness. Show me the plight of the many; let me walk in prayer in the shoes of one person who queues for water, scavenges for food, waits long hours to see a doctor, and lives in a subsiding home.

Week 4

Help me to honour my home, and if necessary to leave it, for your sake and for the sake of your little ones.

PRAYER FOR ACTION

1. *Where lies the vision glorious that moved the saints of old?*
   Where rests the humble piety that made them strong and bold?
   Where throbs the heartfelt aching to renew our spirits cold?
   In our heart where the Spirit prompts.

2. *Our conscience goads us daily at our fellows' poverty;*
   Injustice, war and cruelty are there for all to see.
   Where lies the driving motive that will make all humans free?
   In our world where the Spirit prompts.

3. *But first there lurk within us hidden deep within our soul*
   Fear and anger that divide us and prevent our being whole.
   Whence comes freedom from self-centredness that purifies our goal?
   Through repentance the Spirit prompts.

4. *We would hand in hand with others march in concert with the throng*
   Out of every creed and nation working for a planet strong
   In the century that beckons – Oh! Beat now the starting gong!
   To the sound that the Spirit prompts.

5. *The earth herself drums out a tune in unison with ours;*
   The heavens add their anthem to the sea's pulsating powers.
   God's kingdom's on the move – in hearts and hills and stars –
   Through his Son whom the Spirit prompts.

6. *Forgive us, Lord, our selfishness that spurns your burning love;*
   O'erlook our spiritual weakness that's afraid the world to move.
   Brace us for supreme adventure that is fuelled from above
   By your power that the Spirit prompts.

7. *What a time to live is this in which you work to make things new*
   In a world forlorn yet blessed, tired out yet made anew,
   By the insight of your Gospel that brings rebirth to us too
   In your truth that the Spirit prompts.

8. *Glory, honour, power and blessing be to you, O mighty Lord,*
   Blissful Lover, supreme Giver, flowing Joy, abounding Word!
   Fill us full of love for others from your ever-flowing gourd
   In our heart where the Spirit prompts.

Week 4

CONTEMPLATION

Death, where is your sting, where is your anything?

Week 4

Sunday

I realise, O Lord, the quiet music, the moving solitude of your presence that kindles love within me.

PRAISE

1. *O heavenly King,*
   Look down from above!
   Assist us to sing
   Thy mercy and love:
   So sweetly o'erflowing,
   So plenteous the store,
   Thou still art bestowing,
   And giving us more.

2. *O God of our life,*
   We hallow thy name!
   Our business and strife
   Is thee to proclaim;
   Accept our thanksgiving
   For creating grace;
   The living, the living
   Shall show forth thy praise.

3. *Our Father and Lord,*
   Almighty are thou;
   Preserved by thy word,
   We worship thee now,
   The bountiful donor
   Of all we enjoy!
   Our tongues to thine honor,
   And lives we employ.

4. *But Oh! above all*
   Thy kindness we praise,

Week 4

From sin and from thrall
Which saves the lost race;
Thy Son thou hast given
A world to redeem,
And bring us to heaven,
Whose trust is in him.

5. *Wherefore of thy love*
   We sing and rejoice,
   With angels above
   We lift up our voice;
   Thy love each believer
   Shall gladly adore,
   Forever and ever,
   When time is no more.

~ Charles Wesley[19] ~

THANKS

O God, I give you thanks, with a full heart, for all your goodness.

I bless you for my fellow creatures on this planet: for the sun and its life-giving rays, for the moon and stars, which light up the heavens, for the wind and rain and atmosphere and cloud, which sustain our varied life, for all animals great and small, for the beauty of flower, the songs of birds, the shape of mountains, the joy of your creation.

I bless you for the gift of people: for those who minister to me in the daily tasks of life, for those who love me expecting nothing in return, for those who, even now, are thinking about me and praying for me.

I bless you for spiritual gifts – the gift of faith, the gift of hope and the gift of love.

I bless you for your kingdom of love foretold in the world of creatures and people, and begun in my heart.

With a full heart I thank you, Lord, for all your goodness.

SELF-EXAMINATION AND FORGIVENESS

Forgive me, O Lord, that so often I have received your many gifts with little thanks. Forgive me that so often I have not been moved by the plenitude of your love. Forgive me that so often I have been left cold by the plight of others, by Golgotha and Calvary, because I was too bound up with myself.

Forgive my weakness, O Lord. If I have not been notable in wrongdoing, neither have I been valiant for the right. Show me the true meaning of my coldness of heart, the semi-chaos within.

Week 4

How could I love others as myself if I did not know myself? How could I give myself to you for the sake of others if the self that I would give was a storm-tossed cork? Show me, as my soul can bear, who I am, and grant that, in my looking at one self which I know, I may see through your eyes the self that you would have me be – and may my heart rejoice!

To be converted, to be regenerated, to receive grace, to experience religion, to gain an assurance, are so many phrases which denote the process, gradual or sudden, by which a self hitherto divided, and consciously wrong, inferior and unhappy, becomes unified and consciously right, superior and happy, in consequence of its firmer hold upon religious realities.

~ William James[20] ~

1. *Open, Lord, my inward ear,*
   And bid my heart rejoice!
   Bid my quiet spirit hear
   Thy comfortable voice,
   Never in the whirlwind found,
   Or where earthquakes rock the place;
   Still and silent is the sound,
   The whisper of thy grace.

2. *From the world of sin, and noise,*
   And hurry, I withdraw;
   For the small and inward voice
   I wait, with humble awe.
   Silent am I now, and still,
   Dare not in thy presence move;
   To my waiting soul reveal
   The secret of thy love.

3. *Thou hast undertook for me,*
   For me to death wast sold;
   Wisdom in a mystery
   Of bleeding love unfold;
   Teach the lesson of thy cross,
   Let me die with thee to reign,
   All things let me count but loss
   So I may thee regain.

4. *Show me, as my soul can bear,*
   The depth of inbred sin,
   All the unbelief declare,
   The pride that lurks within;
   Take me, whom thyself hast bought,
   Bring into captivity
   Every high aspiring thought
   That would not stoop to thee.

Week 4

5. *Lord, my time is in thy hand,*
   My soul to thee convert;
   Thou canst make me understand,
   Though I am slow of heart;
   Thine, in whom I live and move,
   Thine the work, the praise is thine,
   Thou art wisdom, power, and love –
   And all thou art is mine.

~ Charles Wesley[21] ~

MEDITATION

If I speak in the tongues of men and of angels, but have not love, I am only a resounding gong or a clanging symbol. If I have the gift of prophecy and can fathom all mysteries and all knowledge, and if I have faith that can move mountains, but have not love, I am nothing. If I give all I possess to the poor and surrender my body to the flames, but have not love, I gain nothing.

Love is patient, love is kind. It does not envy, it does not boast, it is not proud. It is not rude, it is not self-seeking, it is not easily angered, it keeps no record of wrongs. Love does not delight in evil but rejoices with the truth. It always protects, always trusts, always hopes, always perseveres.

Love never fails. But where there are prophecies, they will cease; where there are tongues, they will be stilled; where there is knowledge, it will pass away. For we know in part and we prophesy in part, but when perfection comes, the imperfect disappears. When I was a child, I talked like a child, I thought like a child, I reasoned like a child. When I became a man, I put childish ways behind me. Now we see but a poor reflection as in a mirror; then we shall see face to face. Now I know in part; then I shall know fully, even as I am fully known.

And now these three remain: faith, hope and love. But the greatest of these is love.

~ 1 Corinthians 13 ~

Love is the greatest thing in the world – that is the message of this famous passage. Paul's resounding answer to the perennial question, what is the greatest good?, is quite simply that love is the greatest thing of all. It is greater than the gift of oratory, the ability to convince by eloquence of speech; it is greater than the gift of faith, even though this be deep enough to perform miracles; it is greater than the ecstasy of the prophet, the depth of the mystic, and the realisation of the scholar; it is greater than the highest act of charity or the bravest deed of martyrdom. It is the pearl of greatest price.

Love, in its turn, can be broken up into smaller constituent parts. Henry Drummond applied to it the telling analogy of the prism or the rainbow. Like a light beam put through a prism, or like a rainbow appearing on the horizon, split up into constituent colours of red, blue, yellow, purple, orange, and so on – so love can be split up into its different

Week 4

elements. Love is patient – patience; love is kind – kindness; it does not envy – generosity; it does not boast, it's not proud – humility; it is not rude – courtesy; it is not self-seeking – unselfishness; it is not easily angered – equanimity; it keeps no records of wrongs – forgiveness; it does not delight in evil but rejoices in the truth – authenticity. Whole books could be written on each of these elements of love. They are part of a greater whole; they point back to their source. They are shown in the hurly-burly of everyday life as traits of character; they are cultivated inwardly while appearing outwardly.

At the end of the era, other things will fade away, but love will last. It will last forever. For love is the fulfilment of the law. It is the fulfilment of many other excellent things which, because they are earth-bound, are partial. In short, God is love. Let us therefore treasure love, and treasure God. For where our treasure is, there our heart is also.

PETITION

Lord, make me an instrument of your peace.
Where there is hatred, let me sow love;
Where there is injury, pardon;
Where there is doubt, faith;
Where there is despair, hope;
Where there is darkness, light;
Where there is sadness, joy.
O Divine Master, grant that
I may not so much seek
To be consoled, as to console;
Not so much to be understood as
To understand; not so much to be
Loved as to love:
For it is in giving that we receive;
It is in pardoning that we are pardoned;
It is in dying that we awaken to eternal life.

~ Attributed to St Francis of Assisi ~

PRAYER FOR ACTION

And as he has the strongest affection for the fountain of all good, so he has the firmest confidence in him; a confidence which neither pleasure or pain, neither life nor death, can shake. But yet this, far from creating sloth or indolence, pushes him on to the most vigorous industry. It causes him to put forth all his strength in obeying him in whom he confides; so that he is never faint in his mind, never weary of doing whatever he believes to be his will. And he is continually labouring to transcribe into himself all his imitable perfections: in particular, his justice, mercy, and truth, so eminently displayed in all his creatures. Above all, remembering that God is love, he is conformed to the same likeness.

Week 4

He is full of love to his neighbour: of universal love, not confined to one sect or party, not restrained to those who agree with him in opinions, or in outward modes of worship, or to those who are allied to him by blood or recommended by nearness of place. Neither does he love those only that love him, or that are endeared to him by intimacy of acquaintance. But his love resembles that of him whose mercy is over all his works. It soars above all these scanty bounds, embracing neighbours and strangers, friends and enemies; yes, not only the good and gentle but also the froward, the evil and unthankful. For he loves every soul that God has made, every child of man, of whatever place or nation. And yet this universal benevolence does in nowise interfere with a peculiar regard for his relations, friends, and benefactors, a fervent love for his country and the most endeared affection to all men of integrity, of clear and generous virtue . . .

And this universal, disinterested love is productive of humanity, courtesy, and affability. It makes a Christian rejoice in the virtues of all, and bear a part in their happiness at the same time that he sympathises with their pains and compassionates their infirmities. It creates modesty, condescension, prudence – together with calmness and evenness of temper. It is the parent of generosity, openness, and frankness, void of jealousy and suspicion. It begets candour and willingness to believe and hope whatever is kind and friendly of every man; and invincible patience, never overcome of evil, but overcoming evil with good . . .

The same love is productive of all right actions. It leads him into an earnest and steady discharge of all social offices, of whatever is due to relations of every kind: to his friends, to his country and to any particular community whereof he is a member. It prevents his willingly hurting or grieving any man. It guides him into a uniform practice of justice and mercy, equally extensive with the principle whence it flows. It constrains him to do all possible good, of every possible kind, to all men; and makes him invariably resolved in every circumstance of life to do that, and that only, to others, which supposing he were himself in the same situation, he would desire they should do to him . . .

He is peculiarly and inexpressibly happy in the clearest and fullest conviction: 'This all-powerful, all-wise, all-gracious Being, this Governor of all, loves ME. This lover of my soul is always with me, is never absent; no, not for a moment. And I love him: there is none in heaven but thee, none on earth that I desire beside thee! And he has given me to resemble himself; he has stamped his image on my heart. And I live unto him: I do only his will; I glorify him with my body and my spirit. And it will not be long before I shall die unto him, I shall die into the arms of God. And then . . . it only remains that I should live with him forever.'

~ John Wesley[22] ~

CONTEMPLATION

God is love.

~ 1 John 4:8 ~

Week 4

NOTES

1. Masai Creed – see *Heart of Prayer* (op. cit.), p. 25.
2. John Donne (1573–1631), 'Sonnet' – see *Batsford Book of Religious Verse* (op. cit.), p. 23.
3. Molinos, 'The Spiritual Guide', quoted in Francis B. James, *For the Quiet Hour* (London: Epworth Press, 1952), p. 13.
4. N. Myers (ed.) (op. cit.), p. 258.
5. Adapted from a prayer by Queen Salote of Tonga.
6. Christina Rossetti (1830–94), 'St Peter' – see *The New Oxford Book of Christian Verse*, p. 249.
7. Laurence Housman, 'A Prayer for the Healing of the Wounds of Christ' – see *English Religious Verse* (op. cit.), p. 266.
8. Ernst Lange (1650–1727), trans. by John Wesley (1703–91), alt. by Rupert E. Davies (1909–) – see *Hymns and Psalms* (op. cit.), Hymn 54.
9. Arthur Hugh Clough (1819–61), 'With Whom is no Variableness, Neither Shadow of Turning' – see *English Religious Verse* (op. cit.), p. 222.
10. John Henry Newman (1801–90) – see *Hymns and Psalms* (op. cit.), Hymn 67.
11. Charles Wesley – see *Hymns and Psalms* (op. cit.), Hymn 300.
12. John Bunyan, *The Pilgrim's Progress* – see Francis B. James (op. cit.), p. 22.
13. Narayan Vaman Tilak (1862–1919), trans. by Nicol MacNicol (1870–1952) – see *Hymns and Psalms* (op. cit.), Hymn 539.
14. Dostoievsky, adapted from *The Brothers Karamazov* – see Greene and Gollancz (op. cit.), p. 95.
15. Rabi'a – see A. J. Arberry, *Sufism* (op. cit.), p. 43.
16. Charles Wesley – see the volume by Frank Whaling (ed.) on John and Charles Wesley in the *Classics of Western Spirituality* (New York: Paulist Press), pp. 206–7.
17. John Masefield, 'The Everlasting Mercy' – see *The Collected Poems of John Masefield* (op. cit.), p. 129.
18. St Augustine – see Greene and Gollancz (op. cit.), p. 178.
19. Charles Wesley – see *Hymns and Psalms* (op. cit.), Hymn 504.
20. William James, *The Varieties of Religious Experience* (London: Longman, Green & Co., 1911), p. 189.
21. Charles Wesley – see *Hymns and Psalms* (op. cit.), Hymn 540.
22. John Wesley, 'The Portrait of a Christian', in the volume by Frank Whaling (ed.) on John and Charles Wesley in the *Classics of Western Spirituality* (op. cit.), pp. 122–5.

Week 4